Boundless Imagination of a Child

十岁成长记录画册

Album of My First Ten Years

程莲子

Cheng Lianzi

羊城晚报出版社

·广 州·

图书在版编目（CIP）数据

童心无限 / 程莲子著 . —广州：羊城晚报出版社，2015.12

ISBN 978-7-5543-0275-0

Ⅰ. ①童… Ⅱ. ①程… Ⅲ. ①程莲子—自传—画册 Ⅳ. ① K828.4-64

中国版本图书馆 CIP 数据核字（2015）第 294793 号

童心无限

Tongxin Wuxian

责任编辑 黄初镇
责任技编 张广生
装帧设计 全程設計工廠 何伟权 陈瑜蓉
书名题字 程小宏
责任校对 杨 群
出版发行 羊城晚报出版社（广州市天河区黄埔大道中 309 号羊城创意产业园 3-13B 邮编：510665）
网址：www.ycwb-press.com
发行部电话：（020）87133824
出 版 人 吴 江
经　　销 广东新华发行集团股份有限公司
印　　刷 广州市四维印刷有限公司
规　　格 787 毫米 ×1092 毫米 1/12 印张 22 字数 100 千
版　　次 2015 年 12 月第 1 版 2015 年 12 月第 1 次印刷
书　　号 ISBN 978-7-5543-0275-0/K · 66
定　　价 96.00 元

Contents

你 养 我 长 大　　我 陪 你 变 老

You are the ones who bring me up and I will always be there when you are getting old

纯真与天趣

——读程莲子绘画有感

记得多年前国外做过一次有趣的实验，就是把一批小朋友的画和已经功成名就的画家作品隐去姓名签字，放在拍卖行里让人来竞投。其拍卖结果让人吃惊：不少小朋友的画并未输于名家的画，甚至个别的画还远远高出名家的画价。有记者采访竞投者，得到的答复是：他们并未冲着绘画的作者而去，而是完全看中绘画本身。很多小朋友的画里表现了一种人类共同的天性，一种纯净的、没有经过文明塑造与洗涤的原生态艺术。当我看到程莲子这批画时，让我又一次想起了这个耐人寻味的竞拍。

看到莲子的画，我依然想到的是孩提时代的美好时光。每一个人，与生俱来都有一种天然的艺术基因，只是或多或少而已。有的人经过后天的学习、引导，艺术才能得到充分的发挥，便走向艺术之路；有的人一直未能得到施展，甚至连尝试的机会都没有，因而一直未能与艺术结缘。显然，莲子是幸运的，也是幸福的。她父亲是画家，母亲又是一位知书达理的大家闺秀，从小在这样的家庭环境中，耳濡目染，自然也就有充分的机会展现其艺术的一面。当大多数小朋友还在疯玩之时，她已拿起笔来，在画纸上涂鸦，这极大程度地将她的艺术的潜质释放出来。她没有师承，没有临摹，没有受过任何条条框框的约束，恰好这正是其优势的一面。在她的画里，我们看到不一样的艺术世界：五彩斑斓的树木、奇形怪状的人物、变形夸张的鸟雀、硕大无比的刺猬、杂乱无章的游鱼、鲜艳夺目的荷花、可爱顽皮的小鸭、匪夷所思的房子、时髦招展的女孩、腾空飞翔的气球、五颜六色的池塘、表情怪异的头像、神奇幽怪的花园……孩子的世界，远远比大人的世界要丰富多彩。她的眼中，看到的一切都是彩色的。她的画笔下的各种颜色，不是忠实于物象本色，而是她所理解的孩童世界的原色。这些色彩，构成了她的绘画的主旋律，同时又成其童年时光的一段美好记忆。

我曾经对尚在幼年的女儿说过，只要你想画画，你就随便画，想到什么就画什么，想怎么画就怎么画，哪怕只是在墙上的胡乱涂鸦，都会是一件无与伦比的艺术佳作。如今，我看到莲子的画，我又想起自己曾经说过的这段话。的确，孩子的世界没有大人的世界那么纷繁复杂。他们没有经历人生的风雨，没有世故，甚至没有多余的想法。在他们的世界，有的只是无邪与天真，有的只是五颜六色的童话世界，所以在这样纯净的年龄，落笔必然就是一件件大人们无法企及的佳作。

看到莲子的画，会让人想起很多。但最多的还是，童年时代的美好记忆。我想，这要感谢莲子的父母，是他们无私的奉献与辛勤的耕耘，给莲子提供这么美好的成长空间，才让我们有机会看到莲子的成长足迹，让我们领略到莲子多姿多彩的童年时光。

人生有很多段不同时光。不同的阶段有着不一样的精彩。莲子在人生的初始阶段，便开启其多彩的篇章。她刚刚度过十岁的生日。当然，很快会有二十岁、三十岁……相信有着这段五彩的时光垫底，后来的时光也必将展现出别样的辉煌。

祝愿莲子，祝福莲子！

朱万章

2015 年 12 月于京城景山寓所

（朱万章博士：中国国家博物馆学术研究中心研究馆员、中国美术家协会理论委员会委员、中山大学特聘教授）

Foreword

Innocence and Natural Delight

——After viewing Lianzi's paintings

I remember an interesting experiment conducted years ago in a foreign country. It involved an array of paintings drawn by young children and established painters. The names of the painters were concealed before the paintings were put up for auction. Much to people's surprise, many of the children's paintings turned out more welcomed than the famous painters', some with even higher prices. When interviewed, some bidders said that what they valued most was not the painters but the paintings. Children's paintings represented human nature, which were pure and free from the shaping of civilization. That was the original state of art. The paintings of Lianzi remind me of that interesting auction.

Lianzi's pictures make me think of the happy times of childhood. Every person is more or less born with artistic genes. Some people's talent is brought out and fully tapped through learning and conducting after birth. While the others will never, even without a chance to try, put their natural gift into use. They are likely to end up with no association with art throughout their life time. Apparently, Lianzi is lucky and happy. Her father is a painter and her mother is a well educated elegant lady. Born and brought up in such a family, Lianzi has been influenced by what she sees and hears. And she certainly has the opportunity to develop her artistic talant. While most young children were playing around wildly, Lianzi was holding a painting brush and making graffiti on paper, liberating her artistic potential to a great extent. She has neither had professional training nor try imitating others' paintings. It was the freedom from rules that gave her special advantage. In her paintings, we can see a different world: colorful trees, curiously-shaped people, exaggerated birds and huge hedgehogs, chaotic fish, bright-colored lotuses, naughty ducks, unthinkable houses and wonderful gardens... The world of child is much more colorful than that of an adult. In her eyes, everything is colorful. The color under her brush is not the same as the color of a real object but the color of a child's world in her understanding. All these colors constitute the major theme of her paintings as well as a beautiful memory of her childhood.

I once told my little daughter to draw as she liked whenever she wanted to. She could paint whatever in her mind in any possible way. Even though she made graffiti on the wall, it would be regarded as an incomparable masterpiece of art. When I was watching Lianzi's paintings, I recalled what I said to my daughter. It is true that children's world is not as complicated as that of adults. They haven't experienced the ups and downs of life. They are far from sophisticated. They don't even have much to think about. Their little world is filled with innocence, pureness and a colorful fairy land. At such an age of simplicity, every drawing is sure to become fine art that adults can never accomplish.

The paintings of Lianzi arouse various sentiments, mostly fantastic memories of one's childhood. I think this is to be attributed to her parents who have made selfless sacrifices and constant efforts to provide Lianzi with such admirable growth environment, which enables us to see the way Lianzi has come along and to share her wonderful childhood memories.

There are several periods in one's life, with each one presenting a different kind of splendidness. Lianzi has opened a bright page of her life at the very beginning. She has just become ten years old and surely, she will embrace her twentieth and thirtieth birthdays. I believe that with this period of wonderful time as a foundation, her coming years must be uniquely glorious.

Best wishes and regards to Lianzi!

Zhu Wanzhang

Jingshan Apartment, Beijing, Dec. 2015

(Dr. Zhu Wanzhang: Researcher of the Academic Research Center of National Museum of China,
Member of the Theoretical Committee of Chinese Artists Association,
Distinguished Professor of Sun Yat-Sen University)

爸爸妈妈的话

莲子，爸妈记得……

莲子，爸妈记得，那是在 2006 年的夏天，爸爸在广东画院展览作品，妈妈抱着你观看爸爸画的荷花，你瞪大眼睛好奇地看着，不时伸出小手指着画“呀呀”叫，我们不知是什么拨动了你的兴趣……那年，你还不到一岁！

莲子，爸妈记得，那是在 2007 年的春天，你刚学会走路，就经常蹒跚地爬上爸爸的画台，翻看那些你无法搬动的画册，搬弄那些比你手指还粗的画笔，对五颜六色的颜料充满兴趣。“我要笔笔！我要画画！”你随手抓起毛笔，沾上水墨就在宣纸上乱涂一番，现在还保留了五幅当时的“画作”。那年，你才一岁多！

莲子，爸妈记得，那是在 2008 年北京奥运会期间，妈妈带着你看画展，刚进展厅，被阿姨抱着的你突然兴奋得稚声大叫：“方楚雄！方楚雄！”众人愣了一会才反应过来，原来画壁上挂着两幅方楚雄老师的画作。当时的你连字都不认得，怎么竟能辨认出方老师的作品？妈妈百思不解。也许，是因为你常常喜欢翻看爸爸书柜的画册，对方老师的工笔花鸟特别感兴趣。但是从画风就可以辨认出作者，就算成年人也不容易啊。那年，你才两岁多！

莲子，爸妈记得，接下来的两年里，你突然迸发出极大的兴趣和激情，画了许许多多的画，其中显露的想象力之奇特和表现力之丰富，让我们感到惊讶。那幅《妈妈和宝宝》，妈妈微闭的双眼和宝宝圆睁的好奇眼睛形成鲜明对比；那幅《小鱼鱼》将小姑娘追看小鱼时的兴奋表情和跃动身姿表现得惟妙惟肖；那幅《妈妈生气了》，妈妈生气的神态和宝宝委屈的表情让人忍俊不禁……那时，你才三四岁！

莲子，爸妈记得，从小你就特别喜欢书，每次带你去商场买玩具，你只要看到书就一屁股坐下，拿起各种各样的书看得入迷，最后，带回家的都是一大摞小人书。你从一岁开始陆续阅读了大量的童话和卡通故事，那时候，你连字都还不怎么认得！2011 年的秋天，还不到六岁的你告别了幼儿园，成了汇景实验小学的学生。这期间，你的画中充满了童话故事、海底世界的各种人物、动物、美人鱼……你用色彩缤纷的绘画，展现了对这些童话故事的感悟与想象，展现了对身边的人和事、周围环境的认识，更展现了你对一个美丽世界的好奇和憧憬！

莲子，爸妈记得，那是 2012 年年末和 2013 年年初，爸爸在北京中国美术馆举办名为《荷语》的个人画展，你特意画了一幅画，画面是一幢写着“中国美术馆”的楼房，上面飘着彩色气球，旁边是高高的阶梯，下面是绽放的荷花和绿叶，一个满脸带笑的小姑娘捧着五彩花篮站在门口，画中“祝爸爸画展成功”七个幼嫩的字，倾注了你充满童真的心声。你将这幅画带到了爸爸画展的开幕式上，爸爸高兴地将它摆放在中国美术馆展厅的大门前，看画展的叔叔阿姨逗趣地说：“小莲子的画摆上中国美术馆啦！”……那年，你七岁了。

莲子，爸妈记得，那是 2014 年的秋天，妈妈带你去到大洋彼岸的美国，走进了旧金山亚洲艺术博物馆、斯坦福大学艺术博物馆、洛杉矶盖蒂博物馆等著名艺术展区，你睁大惊奇的眼睛，细细端详那一幅幅触动人心的名家大作，在艺术的殿堂里流连忘返。妈妈清楚地记得，在洛杉矶参观盖蒂博物馆时，你对凡·高的作品《鸢尾花》情有独钟，驻足久看。画面中的鸢尾花没有整齐一律的生长方向，显得凌乱却又有一个共同的近似于挣扎的姿态，像是想挣脱某种无形的束缚。凡·高的一生都在痛苦与挣扎中度过，这幅被誉为凡·高在“圣雷米时期最伟大作品之一”的名画，是其内心那种孤独、挣扎与向往的写照。但这种交织着人生苦涩与充满着蓬勃生机的艺术作品，为何会吸引了你？这时，你还不到九岁！

莲子，爸妈清楚地知道，今年 10 月 8 日，你满十周岁了，这是你人生的一个里程碑。这天，妈妈特意送给你一束灿烂的鲜花和 10 只你最喜欢的熊宝宝。这一年，妈妈带你去香港参观国际著名的巴塞尔艺术大展；去澳洲参观墨尔本维多利亚国家美术馆；在广州参观国家博物馆副馆长陈履生伯伯的画展、书法展、摄影展。这一年，你进入了广东美术馆艺术培训中心接受绘画培训，你一如既往痴迷于画画，作品的表现已大有长进，从不知所云的涂鸦到可表情达意的造型，从简单稚嫩的色块到工整流畅的线条，成长的轨迹清晰可见。在整理你的资料时，我们惊异地发现，这些年里你的各种绘画作品竟然达到了 2000 多幅！并且你还开始喜欢上摄影、服装设计，在这些方面显露出可喜的艺术潜质，这令我们甚感欢欣！因此，爸妈决意为你出版一本成长记录画册——《童心无限》，将你这十年的成长经历和艺术学习记录下来，意在留给你将来一个美好的记忆。也希望你能记住，在你的成长历程中，有不少的人包括亲人、长辈、老师、朋友……为你无私付出，倾注关爱！同时，也让大家分享你创作的快乐，生活的快乐！

莲子，爸妈永远记得，这十年间你成长的每一步足迹，你艺术学习的每一次进步，甚至你每一次的旅游参观、每一次的舞台表演、每一次的调皮撒娇、每一次的欢笑哭泣……都像一张张照片深烙在爸妈的记忆里，其实所有这些也反映在你的一幅幅稚气活脱的成长照片和丰富多彩的艺术创作当中。也许在未来的某一天，当你站在一个较高的平台上，重新翻看这本《童心无限》时，你会发现自己曾经是多么幼稚，自己的绘画是多么可笑，但你一定会为自己这十年打下的基础而感幸运，为自己有一个良好的成长环境而感欣慰，为自己能拥有深深爱着你永远为你感到骄傲的父母而感到满满的幸福！

莲子，未来的五年、十年，你将迈上一个更高的人生台阶，“路漫漫其修远兮”，爸妈希望你将来的口了依然充满阳光，内心美丽，健康快乐！不断通过自己的努力，书写你人生更加美丽的又一页。加油，宝贝！

永远爱你的爸爸妈妈

程小琪　廖东玫

2015 年 12 月

A letter from mom and dad

Lianzi, mom and dad still remember......

Lianzi, mom and dad still remember...it was the Summer of 2006 when dad was holding an art exhibition at Guangdong Painting Academy. One day, mom took you there. You stayed so lovely in mom's arms and your big eyes, widely open with full curiosity, were glued to dad's lotuses on paper. From time to time, you pointed those tender fingers to the pictures with childish mumbling "Ah, ah,...". We just wondered what was so interesting in the elfin eyes of our baby. At that time, you were still under one year old.

Lianzi, mom and dad still remember the Spring of 2007 when you began toddling. You, a baby who could not walk steadily, unexpectedly enjoyed climbing up dad's painting desk and pretended to leaf through those bulky picture albums. The poor paintbrushes, which were larger than your fingers, could never avoid your grab and would soon be dipped into the colorful pigments once you gave an order, "I want the brush! I want to paint!" After that, the brushes must be made to dance wildly on the drawing paper. Fortunately, we still keep five of your "masterpieces" created back then. That year, you were under two years old.

Lianzi, mom and dad still remember a day during the 2008 Olympic Games. Mom took you to see an art exhibition. Just upon arrival, your childish and excited cry broke the quietness in the hall. "Fang Chuxiong, Fang Chuxiong!" You repeated. Everyone got confused at first. Then it dawned on us that there were two paintings of Fang Chuxiong hanging on the wall. Can you imagine mom scratching her head? Because she could never figure out how you recognized the works of Mr. Fang when you did not even know a Chinese character? Perhaps such inspiration came from dad's picture albums. Each time you came across Mr. Fang's Gongbi Painting (traditional Chinese meticulous brushwork), you seemed totally fascinated. Even so, it's still incredible that a two-year-old child could recognize who the painter was from the style of the picture, for we all understood that even an adult could hardly do so.

Lianzi, mom and dad still remember that in the next two years, great interest and passion for painting burst into your heart. You kept drawing on and on. Those paintings were the cradle of your distinctive imagination and expressiveness, which were, undoubtedly, to our great surprise. The one named "Mom and Baby" displayed a sharp contrast between the eyes of the two figures: mom's eyes were drooped slightly while the baby's eyes were widely open with thirst for new things. Another picture, "Little Fish", put a lovely girl happily chasing swimming fish before our eyes. Her excited face and bouncing steps were portrayed as vivid as real. In the picture named "Mom's Angry", mom's irritated expression and the baby's wronged look always made people who saw it laugh. That year, you were only three to four years old.

Lianzi, mom and dad still remember how much love you used to have for reading. Each time you were taken to the shopping mall, what would catch your eyes were not toys but books instead. Sitting still, a little bookworm would soon lost itself in the jungle of books. With no exception, you would stagger home loaded with your trophies—a pile of picture-story books. Your journey paved with story books and cartoon stories started from the age of one. But you could hardly do any reading at that time! Then in the Autumn of 2011, younger than six, you bid farewell to kindergarten and became a student at Huijing Experimental Primary School. Afterwards, we discovered in your paintings a wonderland decorated with fairy tales, various figures from the undersea world, especially animals like mermaids... What you felt and imagined about those fairy tales, how you understood the surroundings, what kind of dreams you cherished about a beautiful world were all cast into a colorful world of drawings created by yourself.

Lianzi, mom and dad still remember that at the joint of 2012 and 2013, dad was holding art exhibition ("Lotus Talk") at National Art Museum of China in Beijing. For this, you drew a picture as congratulation gift: The building in the picture was named

"National Art Museum of China". Up to the top, a row of brightly colored balloons were flying. And the towering stair beside was extending high in the air. Move eyes downward and we found the lotuses in delicate red and their verdant leaves; A little girl smiling cheerfully was right standing at the gate of the museum, with a beautiful flower basket in her hand. The words you put on the picture— "Wish dad a successful exhibition" —came out of your sincere heart just to stay in my own. Dad placed it at the entrance of the art museum with full pride. Seeing your work, some of the guests said with humor, "Our little Lianzi is displaying her painting at the National Art Museum of China." You were seven years old on that day.

Lianzi, mom and dad still remember the Autumn of 2014 when you went on a journey with mom to the other side of the Pacific Ocean —the U.S . You visited a couple of famous art exhibition sites like Asian Art Museum in San Francisco, Art Museum of Stanford University and Getty Museum in Los Angeles. From your eyes we could tell that you must have been surprised by the stunning beauty of those art pieces and lost yourself in the paradise of art. Mom clearly recalled the scene that you stopped before Van Gogh's "Flower-De-Luce" for quite a long time in Getty Museum. In that picture, the flowers grew in diverging directions, presenting a posture of struggle and chaos. They gave people the impression that there were about to escape, perhaps a sort of constraint that was invisible. Van Gogh spent his whole life in misery and struggle. Believed to be the portrayal of Van Gogh's loneliness, flounder and hopes, this picture was renowned as "one of the greatest works by Van Gogh during the Saint-Remy Period". But how would such a piece of art intertwined with the sadness of life and flourishing vitality attract you, a child under nine years old?

Lianzi, mom and dad know clearly you have reached a milestone in your life. On October 8th, you became ten years old. Mom gave you a bunch of flowers and ten baby bear toys as gifts. In this special year, mom accompanied you to Art Basel in Hongkong, the National Gallery of Victoria in Melbourne, Australia, and the art exhibition of uncle Chen Lvsheng (Vice Curator of National Museum) in Guangzhou. During this year, you started to learn painting in the Art Training Center of Guangdong Museum of Art. The great passion for drawing has been carried on. And your recent works are showing apparent advances. Unintelligible graffiti became structures that can express emotions and meanings; Simple color lumps turned into smooth lines— all are evident signs of the progresses you have made. While collecting your paintings, to our surprise, the number of your paintings amounted to as many as over 2000. What's more, you gradually fell in love with photography and costume designing, in both of which you must have great talent. We are proud of you! So, mom and dad decided to publish this picture album, *Boundless Imagination of a Child*. It records the past ten years of your life and art study. We hope to cherish the beautiful memories that you will look back in the future. And you need to remember that your family, elders, teachers and friends have given their selfless love and care to you during your growth. Meanwhile, this album shares your happiness in painting and happiness in life with everyone who loves you.

Lianzi, mom and dad will never forget even a minor step you moved forward on the stages of life and art. We will remember every one of your trips and every movement you made on the stage. All your cute coquetries and naughty times will remain fresh in our memory. And all your tears and smiles are just like shining stones inset on our hearts. Actually, all those much valued experiences have been projected in your lovely photos and wonderful artistic creations. Perhaps one day in the future when you become a greater achiever, you will laugh at your childish paintings. Nevertheless, we believe you will realize how lucky you were to have laid such a solid foundation over the first ten years of life, and how happy it was to have grown up in a relatively superior environment with parents who treated you as the apple of their eye and who always felt so proud of you.

Lianzi, if life is a ladder, you will reach a higher platform in the coming five to ten years. Just as our ancient wisdom indicates, "The road forward will be a long one and is not without difficulty". Mom and dad hope your future life can be enlightened by sunshine, and your beautiful heart is always taken care of. Wish you good health and joy forever! And never stop working hard to write a brighter page in your own book of life. Baby, nothing is to be afraid of!

Love you forever, mom and dad
Cheng Xiaoqi, Liao Dongmei
Dec. 2015

2006 · 襁褓

Swaddle

好开心 Happiness, Burst!

清澈的目光，第一次接触多彩的世界
稚嫩的小手，第一次抓紧他们的双手
高大的爸爸
撑起一片坚实屋檐，为我遮风挡雨
漂亮的妈妈
编织一个温馨摇篮，让我四季如春

Crystal eyes
Had the first glance of the colorful world
Chubby hands
Took the first hold of parents' hands
My father, tall and strong
Protects me from wind and rain
My mother, pretty and elegant
Makes me a warm cradle that feels like the eternity of Summer's Day

看书书 Reading Book

和著名画家杨之光爷爷（左三）在一起
With My Dearest Painter-Mr. Yang Zhiguang (third from left)

妈咪抱我参观爸爸画展
Mom’ s Arms-I-Dad’ s Exhibition

我是小小指挥家 I am a little musical conductor

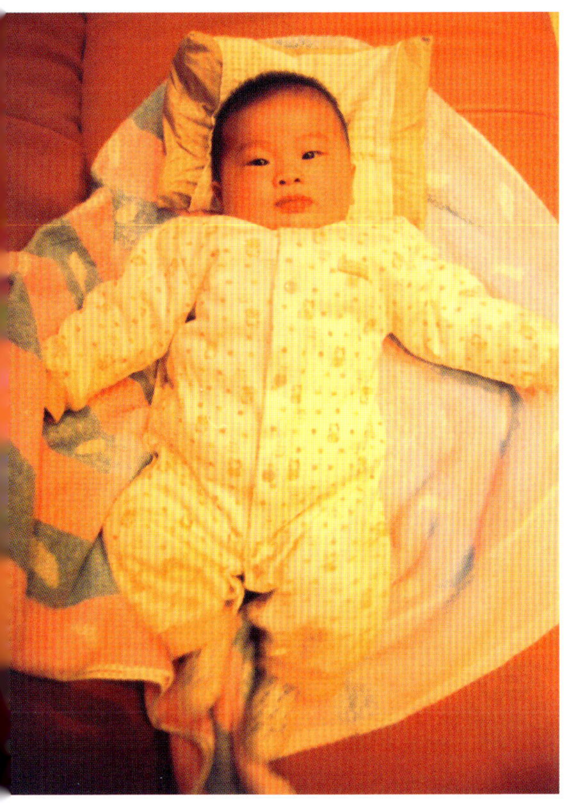

好温暖 How warm it is !

舅爷叫我“胖小弟” Granduncle calls me “chubby boy”

穿花裙，吃手手 Floral Skirt and Yummy Fingers

成长照片

Photos of Different Growth Phases

舅舅背背我

Dear Uncle, Mr. Horse

娃哈哈
Wahaha

摇呀摇，摇到外婆桥　Flickering to“Grandma Bridge”

亲爱的外婆　Dear Grandma

我 1 岁啦
My First Birthday!

广东省妇幼保健院儿童保健科早期教育中心

测试单位：广东省妇幼保健院儿保科　　合作单位：广东省妇幼保健院

宝宝的基本信息　　测试日期:2006年4月27日

宝宝姓名：程莲子　　性别：女孩子　　年龄：5.9 月　　早教编号：010023　　门诊卡号：2006042701001

神经心理发育测试结果

智力能区	得分	等级
大动作	6	
精细动作	5.5	
适应性行为	6.5	
语言	6	
社交行为	6.5	
发育商	105.39	

潜能开发方案

根据 程莲子 小朋友的发育水平，我们制定了科学的训练方案，希望可以帮助您提高宝宝的发育水平。

项目描述：翻身打滚
训练目标： 提高身体的灵活性以及视听觉与头、颈、躯体、四肢肌肉活动的协调
操作过程：1. 宝宝仰卧，在宝宝的一侧，用玩具逗引他翻身，引导他从仰卧变成俯卧，再从俯卧转成仰卧。2. 这时的宝宝，已经有
足够的能力自己翻身，妈妈无需帮助，尽量让宝宝自己翻身打滚。

项目描述：蹦蹦跳
训练目标： 发展下肢力量，为站立做准备，训练言语与动作的联系能力
操作过程：1. 扶着宝宝腋下站在床上，
举宝宝蹦蹦跳。2. 一边举，一边有节奏地念着[蹦-蹦-跳]，念[跳]的时候，就将宝宝举起来。

项目描述：爬行练习
训练目标： 锻炼宝宝头颈部及背部伸肌运动，促进四肢活动和伸展，增强体质
操作过程：1. 让宝宝俯卧，双腿稍弯曲，你用手心抵住他的足底，使其以腹部为支点向前匍匐爬行，在宝宝的前面，用玩具逗引宝
宝向前够取玩具。2. 大人不要主动推婴儿向前，只需顶住他的足底，尽量让婴儿主动蹬脚。3. 每天练习3～5次，每次5分
钟。

项目描述：独坐
训练目标： 锻炼躯干肌肉的力量和控制身体平衡的能力
操作过程：1. 妈妈坐在地上，两腿分开，抱宝宝坐在两腿中间，让宝宝练习独坐。2. 在宝宝的前面，用玩具逗引，让宝宝练习俯身
拿玩具，然后坐直。3. 用玩具逗引宝宝转身。3. 此时宝宝还坐得不稳，妈妈要注意保护宝宝。

项目描述：婴儿主动体操
训练目标： 锻炼全身肌肉，增强体质
操作过程：第一节扶双臂起坐运动，第二节扶单臂起坐运动，第三节腰部桥形运动，第四节握腕跪起直立运动，第五节提腿运动，
第六节扶肘起立运动，第七节弯腰运动，第八节跳跃运动。

项目描述：婴幼儿游泳
训练目标： 发展触觉，锻炼全身肌肉，促进食欲，改善睡眠，增强体质
操作过程：1. 使用婴幼儿专用的游泳设备。2. 每周1～2次，每次15～20分钟。有条件者可在家里每天游。3. 注意安全，一定要有家
长守护在泳池旁，水温35℃左右。4. 一边游泳，一边听音乐，或唱歌给宝宝听。

项目描述：抓取小东西
训练目标： 锻炼指尖细小肌肉的协调动作
操作过程：经常让宝宝练习抓取黄豆大小的东西，例如小饼干、旺旺小馒头、小米花等，即使吃进口内也会立即溶化的东西。

2007 · 蹒跚

Totterer

涂鸦——乱涂哦 Graffiti- Drawing as I Like

蹒跚地
爬上爸爸的画台
笨拙地
拿起爸爸的画笔
抹出一道道、一块块
哦，我是一个小画家

Staggering up father's drawing board
I took a paintbrush
With clumsy movements
I drew my pictures
With messy lines and shapes
What a painter I came to be

花花草草
Flowers and Grass

红鸭子 Red Duck

长颈鹿的家 The Giraffe's Home

红花花 Red Flowers

小鸟飞飞 Little Flying Birds

成长照片

Photos of Different Growth Phases

涂鸦——真好玩　Graffiti-How Funny!

涂鸦——乱涂哦　Graffiti-Drawing as I Like

涂鸦——歇歇了　Graffiti-Taking a Rest

涂鸦——完成啦　Graffiti-I' m done!

奔跑 Wind Beneath My Feet

这是什么叶子？ Leaf, what’ s your name ?

兰花指 Orchid on My Finger Tips

奔跑 Wind Beneath My Feet

去花园采花花 Picking Flowers in the Garden

在长隆看动物 You guys in Chimelong Safari Zoo, I' m coming!

书书真好看 Books, I love you

发呆 I' m not here

大家都来照个相　Be quick!Come into the picture

我和帅爸靓妈　What a handsome family!

妈妈说我比花美　Mom says I' m more beautiful than flowers. She's right!

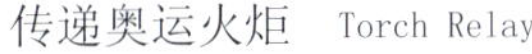
传递奥运火炬　Torch Relay

幼儿园运动会　Kindergarten Sports Day

跑向终点　Running to the End

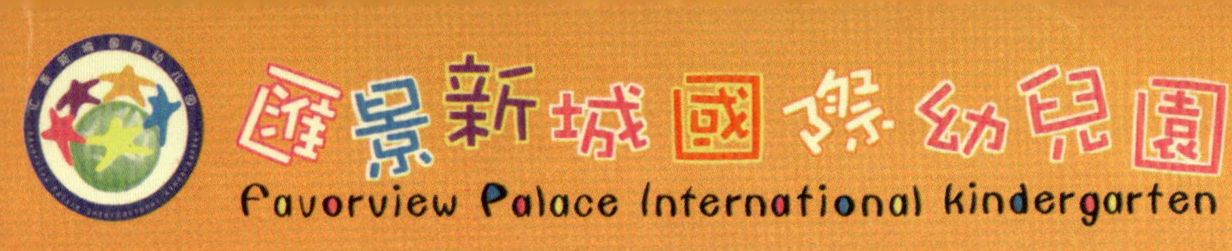

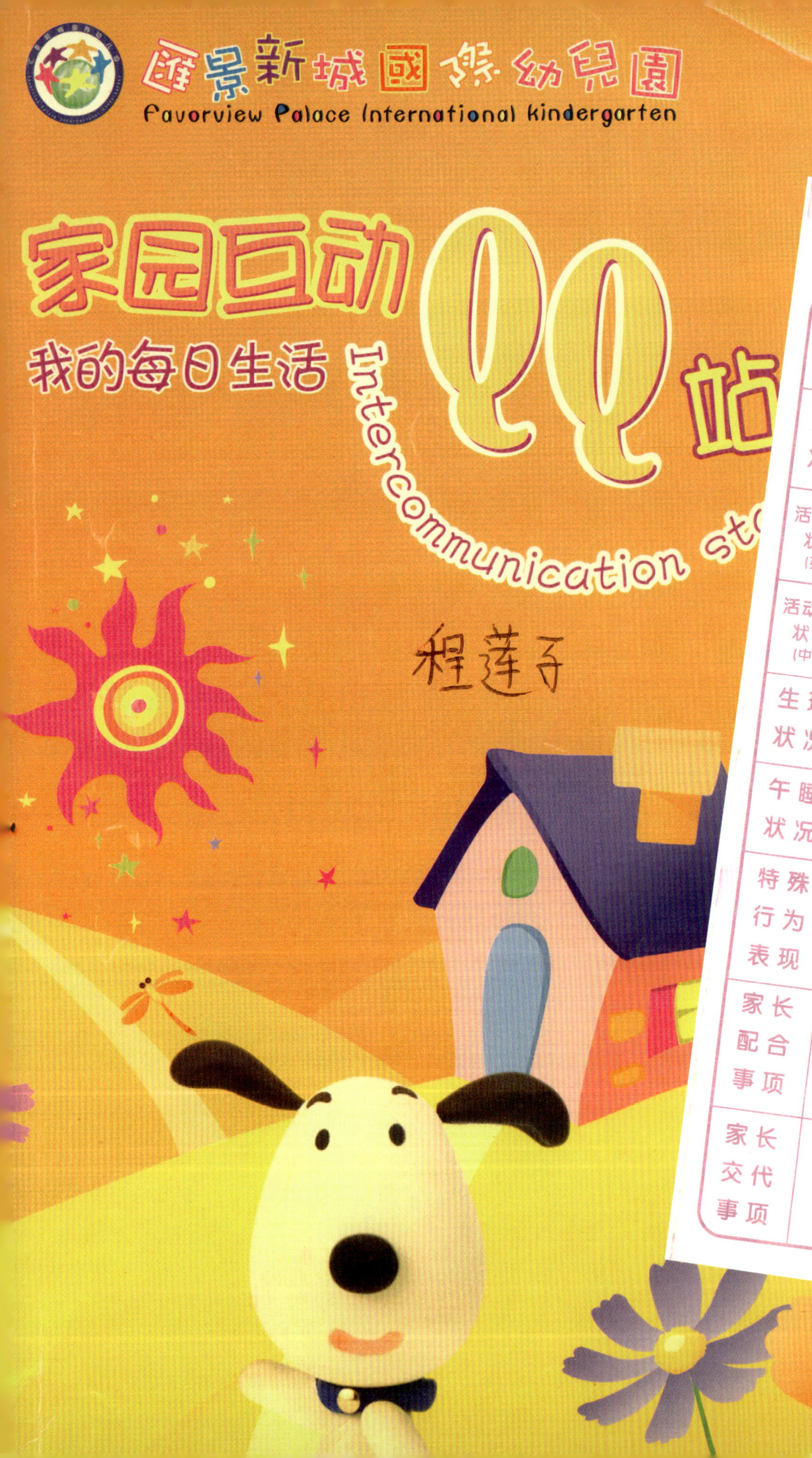
雅景新城國際幼兒園
Favorview Palace International kindergarten
家园互动QQ站
我的每日生活
Intercommunication st
程莲子

日期 2007 年 12 月 6 日 星期 四 记录者：

入园状况	入园时间：(√) 正常 ( ) 迟到 情绪表现：(√) 愉快 ( ) 普通 ( ) 哭闹 ( ) 沮丧 相互问好：(√) 主动 ( ) 被动 ( ) 不理不睬没反应 特殊行为：
用餐状况	早　餐：　午餐：　西点： 食　量：( ) 佳 (√) 正常 ( ) 不佳 速　度：( ) 快 ( ) 正常 (√) 慢 特殊行为：
活动参与状况（英文）	精　神：( ) 佳 (√) 普通 ( ) 不佳 参与度：( ) 主动 (√) 被动 ( ) 没反应 与同学互动：( ) 佳 (√) 普通 ( ) 没互动 特殊行为：
活动参与状况（中文）	精　神：( ) 佳 (√) 普通 ( ) 不佳 参与度：( ) 主动 (√) 被动 ( ) 没反应 与同学互动：( ) 佳 (√) 普通 ( ) 没互动 特殊行为：
生理状况	排便次数：( ) 无 (1) 次 排便时间：(12:00 小便次数：( ) 频繁 (√) 普通 ( ) 少 排汗现象：( ) 多量 (√) 正常 ( ) 很少
午睡状况	午睡时间：( ) 无 (√) 短 ( ) 长 生理表现：(√) 正常 ( ) 咳嗽 ( ) 呼吸不顺 特殊行为：1:30入睡 2:30醒
特殊行为表现	莲子今天情绪不错，愿意自己吃饭，午餐吃得不多，下午吃得较好。上课也能坐着和大家一起学习。
家长配合事项	
家长交代事项	

日期：2007年12月7日 星期五 记录者：

入园状况	入园时间：（√）正常 （ ）迟到 情绪表现：（√）愉快 （ ）普通 （ ）哭闹 （ ）沮丧 相互问好：（ ）主动 （√）被动 （ ）不理不睬没反应 特殊行为：
用餐状况	早 餐： 午餐： 西点： 食 量：（ ）佳 （√）正常 （ ）不佳 速 度：（ ）快 （√）正常 （ ）慢 特殊行为：
活动参与状况（英文）	精 神：（ ）佳 （√）普通 （ ）不佳 参与度：（ ）主动 （√）被动 （ ）没反应 与同学互动：（ ）佳 （√）普通 （ ）没互动 特殊行为：
活动参与状况（中文）	精 神：（ ）佳 （√）普通 （ ）不佳 参与度：（ ）主动 （√）被动 （ ）没反应 与同学互动：（ ）佳 （√）普通 （ ）没互动 特殊行为：
生理状况	排便次数：（√）无 （ ）次 排便时间：（ ） 小便次数：（ ）频繁 （√）普通 （ ）少 排汗现象：（ ）多量 （√）正常 （ ）很少
午睡状况	午睡时间：（ ）无 （√）短 （ ）长 生理表现：（√）正常 （ ）咳嗽 （ ）呼吸不顺 特殊行为：13:15睡，14:30醒
特殊行为表现	莲子今天的表现还不错，精神很好，上厕所有时会说尿尿的，午睡时刚要玩，看书，杨老师给她讲故事，她慢慢就睡了。基本情况还是有进步的。相信每天坚持送她上幼儿园，莲子很快就能适应的。希望家长在家适当给点约束，她知道要听大人的话！！
家长配合事项	
家长交代事项	

日期：2007年12月10日 星期一 记录者：

入园状况	入园时间：（√）正常 （ ）迟到 情绪表现：（√）愉快 （ ）普通 （ ）哭闹 （ ）沮丧 相互问好：（√）主动 （ ）被动 （ ）不理不睬没反应 特殊行为：
用餐状况	早 餐： 午餐： 西点： 食 量：（ ）佳 （ ）正常 （√）不佳 速 度：（ ）快 （ ）正常 （√）慢 特殊行为：
活动参与状况（英文）	精 神：（√）佳 （ ）普通 （ ）不佳 参与度：（ ）主动 （√）被动 （ ）没反应 与同学互动：（ ）佳 （√）普通 （ ）没互动 特殊行为：
活动参与状况（中文）	精 神：（ ）佳 （√）普通 （ ）不佳 参与度：（ ）主动 （√）被动 （ ）没反应 与同学互动：（ ）佳 （√）普通 （ ）没互动 特殊行为：
生理状况	排便次数：（ ）无 （ ）次 排便时间：（ ） 小便次数：（ ）频繁 （√）普通 （ ）少 排汗现象：（ ）多量 （√）正常 （ ）很少
午睡状况	午睡时间：（ ）无 （√）短 （ ）长 生理表现：（√）正常 （ ）咳嗽 （ ）呼吸不顺 特殊行为：
特殊行为表现	莲子对饭菜还是不太喜欢，反而午睡就要吃老师的饭菜。不过今天没拉湿裤子，表扬。但会趁老师不注意，玩水，这样不好哦！
家长配合事项	
家长交代事项	

2008·涂鸦

Graffiti

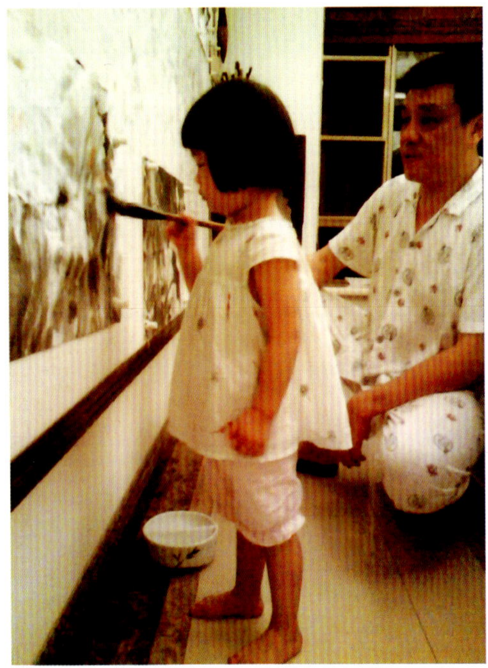

爸爸看我“画画”　Dad watching me “drawing”

拿起沉沉的画笔
涂画出第一幅水彩画
爸爸看着，露出迷惑的目光
“宝宝画的是什么？”
看不懂了吧
那是我，一个小女孩的天空

Holding a heavy paintbrush
I drew my first piece of watercolor
Father was watching in confusion but glamour
What is my baby drawing
A little girl’s painting
Reflecting her inner world so mystifying
That is something you may never know

小鱼鱼真好看　You are pretty, little fish

鱼鱼水中游 Swimming Fish

红色小鱼鱼 Little Fish in Red

彩色海底 The Colorful Undersea World

鱼儿水里游 Swimming Fish

海底尼莫鱼的家　Nemo's House in the Sea

彩色的水渍像什么？　What do these colorful water spots look like？

大嘴巴鱼　Big-Mouth Fish

水母小美美　Jellyfish Mimi

蓝天上，鸟儿飞　Flying Birds in the Blue Sky

《小鲤鱼历险记》里的双面龟、阿酷海马和龙虾、大螃蟹
Two-Sided Turtle, Sea Horse Cool, Lobster and Big Crab in The Adventures of Little Carp

汽车长了两个大眼睛　The car has two big eyes

布娃娃　Rag Doll

戴帽子的小男孩　Boy with a Cap

有爱心的小姑娘　Little Girl Full of Love

我和花儿谁更美？ Who is more beautiful, the flower or me？

成长照片

Photos of Different Growth Phases

小提琴手

Little Fiddler

我和小白兔 Little Rabbit and I

小小班同学　Classmates in Kindergarten

快乐运动会　Happy Sports Day

我爱北京天安门　I love Tian'anmen in Beijing

我是领队　I'm the leader

谭伯伯带我看什么？
What are we looking at, Uncle Tan ?

去鸟巢看奥运　Watching the Olympics in Bird's Nest

北海公园的树林子　The woods in Beihai Park

妈妈看我我看花
Eyes on Me: Mom → I → Flower

弹钢琴 Playing the Piano

数手指 Counting Fingers

小公主 Little Princess

我自己吃饭 Eating by Myself

公　证　书

中华人民共和国北京市方圆公证处

天二十小时二十七分钟的飞行，神舟七号载人飞船返回舱于二〇〇八年九月二十八日十七时三十八分在内蒙古中部地区着陆回收，飞船返回舱于二〇〇八年九月三十日十六时三十分运至中国空间技术研究院。

本公证员与公证员徐敏于二〇〇八年十月一日十时在中国空间技术研究院现场参加了返回舱的开舱过程，将从返回舱中取出的搭载物保存于北京市方圆公证处。二〇〇八年十月七日本公证员和公证人员潘静、中国空间技术研究院工作人员袁辉在北京市方圆公证处开封搭载物品包装袋，并对搭载物进行清点。北京乾迅文化传播有限公司搭载的个性化邮票共151枚，编号自FA001—FA151号；经核对无误后申请人在每枚邮票背面粘贴了带有编号的辨别标识，标识分两部分，一部分粘贴在邮票背面，一部分留存于本公证卷内。

兹证明神舟七号载人飞船返回舱开舱时搭载个性化邮票的包装袋封装情况良好，封条完好无损；并证明带有辨别标识的、编号为FA112号的“祝福”个性化邮票一枚，取自于编号为SZDZ7—16的搭载包装袋，是神舟七号载人飞船搭载物之一；与本公证书相粘连的影印件与该枚个性化邮票原件相符。

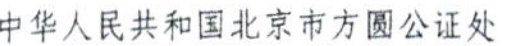
中华人民共和国北京市方圆公证处

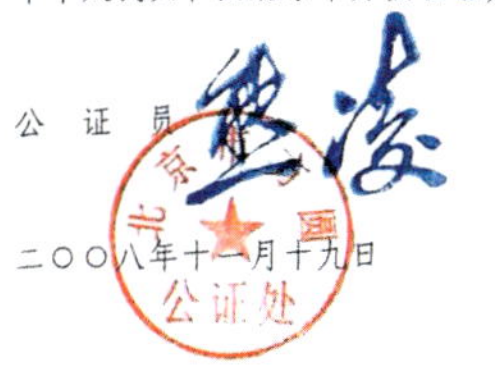
公　证　员

二〇〇八年十一月十九日

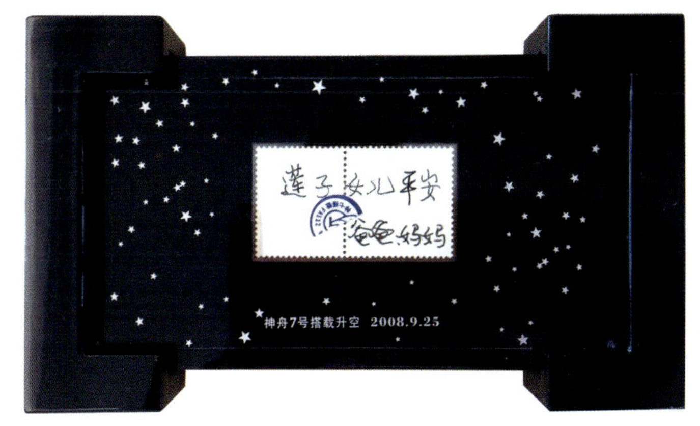

这枚邮票曾搭载神舟七号飞船，跟随宇航员翱翔宇宙，爸爸妈妈在寄托着“祝福”的邮票背面写着“莲子女儿平安”！这是具有特殊意义的纪念邮票，这纪念邮票全世界仅有151枚。

This stamp once travelled with astronauts on the Shenzhou VII Spaceship to the universe. On the back of this much “blessed” stamp, Mom and Dad wrote "Wish our daughter Lianzi a safe life!" Therefore, this special stamp carries memorable meaning. And there are only 151 stamps of the same kind in the world.

匯景新城國際幼兒園
Pavorview Palace Internationaal kindergarten

走进孩子的泡泡世界 传播我们的思想理念 体验师者的心灵触动 共享教育的欢乐境界

汇景新城国际幼儿园主办　2008.7（总第九期）

雪绒花

※《聊天——父母和孩子的“精神脐带”》詹校长专栏
※《家庭成员要形成教育孩子的共同体》园长随笔
※“迎奥运，表童心！”第二届粉笔画大赛
※“用我们的爱点燃希望…”向灾区儿童献爱心系列活动
※ 多才多艺的孩子王·记教师才艺大比拼
※ 不一样的“六·一”儿童节

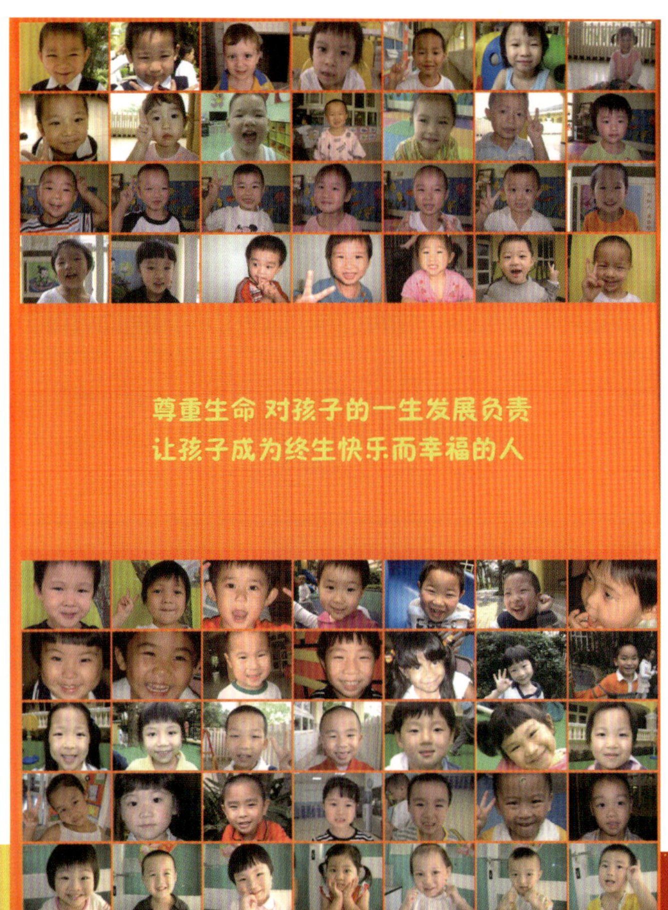

尊重生命 对孩子的一生发展负责
让孩子成为终生快乐而幸福的人

庆“六一”木偶剧表演

CoCo

六一国际儿童节到了！在大家的记忆里，每到六一，孩子们会非常忙，大热的天要排练节目，为的是演给别人或家长看。

今年，我们要过一个不一样的六一！

老师们经过思维碰撞，一下就蹦出一个好点子：木偶剧表演。因为小朋友都喜欢看木偶剧，而且这次是老师表演给小朋友看，在六一这一天，让小朋友好好的当一次观众！欣赏老师们为小朋友带来的“六一礼物”！

26

特别记录

用我们的爱心点燃希望……
汇景新城幼儿园向灾区儿童献爱心系列活动

园长小记

44

2007-2008 年第一学期幼儿评价表

姓名：程莲子　　班别：小 鸭 班　　年龄：2 岁半

项目	内容 评价结果
老师的话：	莲子，虽然来幼儿园的时间不长，但也度过了一个的愉快时光。在这学期里，老师觉得莲子有了不同的变化，言行举止间成长了不少。在课堂上，莲子也会做好与小朋友一起上课，听老师讲课，听到她喜欢的内容时也会大胆说出自己的想法，是有进步的。 莲子还经常带来好看有趣的图书和大家分享。其实莲子的这些学期兴趣很大程度归功于爸爸妈妈对她的正确引导和培养。继续加油吧。 老师还发现莲子比较讲道理，只要老师把道理讲清楚了，莲子都能愉快接受，希望你能尽快的改正吧，养成一个好的品质习惯，答应老师哦！好吗？相信你肯定能做到的。亲爱的宝贝，我为你加油哦！
保育老师的话：	莲子是个可爱的小家伙，来幼儿园才一个多月，在生活自理还是需要老师的帮助，刚来时幼儿园的饭菜基本不吃，到后来慢慢适应了幼儿园的生活，自己会拿图书看，在玩具区里玩的很开心，不喜欢和小朋友一起玩，还需要时间去适应，老师希望下学期回来能看到你和小朋友一起分享玩具。加油哦，小莲子。
外教的话： Foreign Teacher's comment	Lily is a shy little girl, with a beautiful smile. When I turn to ask him a question he becomes quiet and shy. I am sure he will do great in the following semester.

下学期重点培养或重点关注的方面：

莲子很快就要做姐姐了，希望你不再娇气，提高自己的自理能力，做到不但能照顾自己，下学期我们看到一个很棒的莲子，老师知道莲子一定会有更大进步的！

体重（kg）:13.4　身高（cm）:88

评价：中

2007-2008 年第二学期幼儿评价表

姓名：程莲子　　班别：小 鸭 班　　年龄：2 岁半

项目	内容 评价结果
老师的话：	很快又到了学期结束的时候了，莲子其实是一个非常聪明善良的宝宝，经过一个学期，宝宝也喜欢上了幼儿园。宝宝每天都坚持上幼儿园，表扬！虽然宝宝有时上课不够认真，但是每次都能很快把老师教的知识掌握好。希望下个学期宝宝会坐好和其他小朋友一起上课吧！ 宝宝是一个热情大方的孩子，有了好玩好吃的总是想到带来幼儿园和小朋友分享。真棒！小朋友们也都非常喜欢宝宝，宝宝不在的时候，大家都会问，莲子呢？所以宝宝在班上有很多好朋友。 莲子，加油哦！！！
保育老师的话：	莲子：你是个非常活泼开朗的小家伙。很快一个学期过去了，看着你一天天的长大，一天天的懂事，老师真替你高兴噢！现在吃饭也很棒了，开始大口大口的吃了，喝起汤来像在唱歌似的。每天到休息时间就会进睡室里去换鞋子，现在还学会了自己把鞋子摆整齐呢！在游戏中遵守游戏纪律，平时能与同伴友好相处！努力吧，孩子！
外教的话： Foreign Teacher's comment	Apple was better now than before. Now she knows how to listen in the class. She's very young on her age to listen and catch her attention. I am happy to teach Apple. Good Luck.

下学期重点培养或重点关注的方面：

活泼可爱的你让老师疼爱怜惜，聪明的你学会的事情可真多：会自己吃饭，能自己上厕所，能跟着老师唱歌跳舞做早操，还能有礼貌地跟老师问候与道别，真棒！你真是杨妈妈的好宝宝喔！老师衷心的希望新的学期里你更勇敢、更大方！

血色素：138　乙肝表面抗体：0.40　体重：14 公斤　身高：91　评价：中

2009 · 想象

Imagination

看！我的画画 Look, My Drawings

拼拼贴贴
拼出一个个图案
画画写写
画出一张张画图
想象
像一副张开的翅膀
无拘无束
在天上飞翔

Trying and collaging, I make various patterns
Drawing and writing, I do different paintings
Imagination is like a pair of wings
Taking me high in the sky
As free as the breeze

作品点评

垂闭的双眼，对一切都似见怪不怪，熟视无睹——这是妈妈；圆睁的眼睛，对一切都充满好奇，总想探究——这是宝宝。此画的精妙之处就在眼睛，寥寥几笔，就将两代人不同的精神面貌表现得如此形象、准确而传神，非常有趣。

——张建平

Appreciation of Painting

The subtlety of this painting lies in the two figures'eyes. The mother's eyes are drooping, showing not even a slight surprise to anything surrounding. However, the baby's eyes are widely open, showing insatiable curiosity for everything. With just several strokes, the painter portrays different mentalities of the two generations in a lifelike and expressive manner. That's very interesting!

—Zhang Jianping

妈妈和宝宝 Mom and Baby

我和花儿谁更美？
Who is more beautiful, the flower or me ?

穿棉衣、戴帽子的小姑娘
The Little Girl in Cotton-Padded Coat and Hat

戴项链的小女孩　The Little Girl Wearing a Necklace

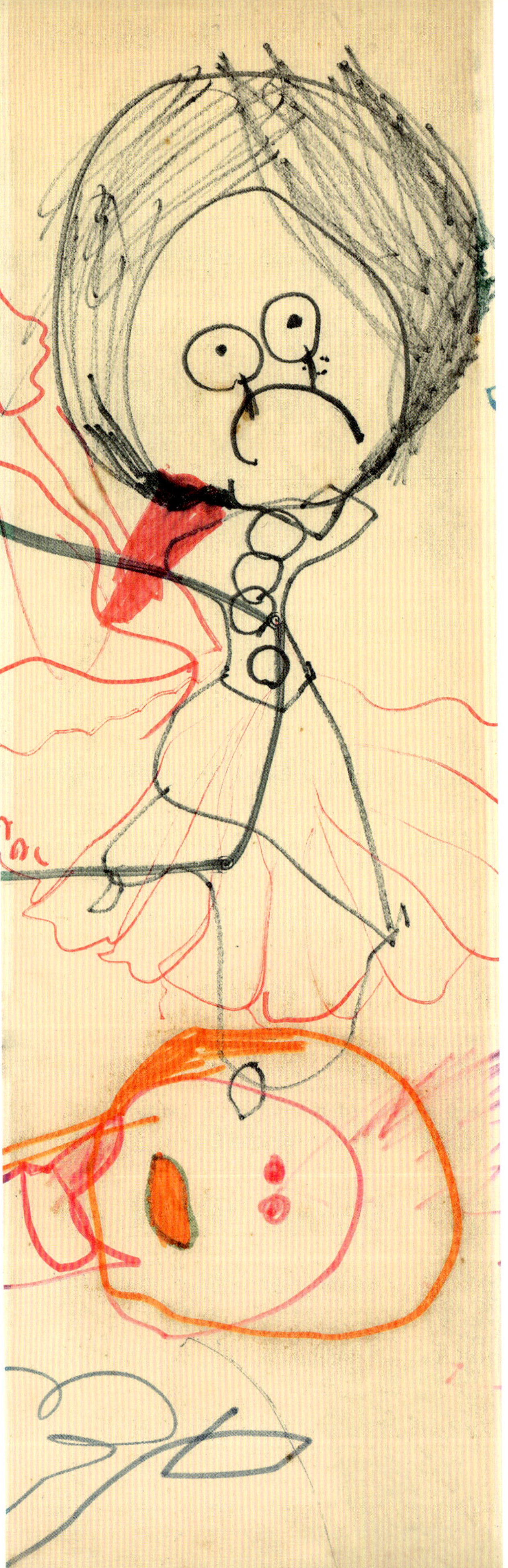

作品点评

妈妈双眼圆睁，嘴巴下撇，一幅生气的神态；宝宝两眼挤在一起，嘴巴似张似闭，委屈的表情跃然纸上，让人忍俊不禁。作画贵在表情达意。一个三岁女孩能将这些表情画得如此逼真和风趣，其观察力和表现力可见一斑。

——张建平

Appreciation of Painting

The value of painting lies in the emotion it conveys. In this picture, the mother, with eyes widely open and lips curled up, is obviously very angry. The child, feeling wronged by her mother, winked her eyes and sobbed with the mouth half closed. How could anyone who sees the picture not be joyfully attracted? These two figures are vividly portrayed by a three-year-old girl. No one would deny her excellent ability to observe and to express people's emotions.

—Zhang Jianping

妈妈生气啦！ Mom is angry!

红苹果香又甜　Red Apple: Fragrant and Sweet

穿黄裙子的美人鱼和小鱼鱼
The Mermaid in Yellow Skirt and the Little Fish

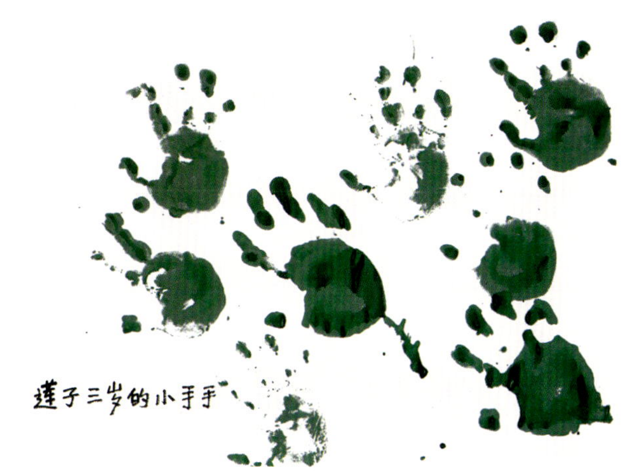

我的小手　My Little Hands

八仙女　Eight Fairies

我们表演服装秀
We are having a fashion show

神气的小娃娃
Perky Little Doll

绿裙子 Green Skirt

跳舞的小女孩 Dancing Girl

荷塘，鱼鱼，小草　Lotus Pond, Fish and Grass

花儿开开，小鸟飞来　Flowers Bloom, Birds Come

母鸡带小鸡　The Hen and Her Children

小鸟和花花　Little Birds and Flowers

祝妈妈节日快乐　Dear mom, happy holiday!

对称的图案像螃蟹？ Isn't it like a crab?

小树结果果　The Fruit on a Small Tree

动物园里的老虎　King of the Forest Trapped in the Zoo

海底世界真有趣　Interesting Undersea World

红鲤鱼　Red Carp

这是什么？ What's this？

鸭妈妈带着鸭宝宝 Mother Duck and Her Baby

水草 Float Grass

果果 Fruits

成长照片

Photos of Different Growth Phases

迪斯科　Disco

盘腿坐，像佛佛　“Cross-legged Buddha”

我自己喝汤，耶！　Drinking soup is so easy...

迪士尼很好玩，耶！　Disney is so fun, yeah!

妈妈教我戴墨镜　Like Mother Like Daughter

百万葵园是我的乐园　Sunflower Garden-My Paradise

学画画 Learning to Draw

画个大苹果 Drawing a Big Apple

拼花花 Making Pieces into Flowers

做贺卡送妈妈 Making a Card for Mom

我走神了 I'm daydreaming

大合唱 Chorus

我是护旗手 Cool Flag Escort

我们去捉鱼 Don't go, fish!

幼儿园的公开课 Public Class in Kindergarten

生日快乐！ Happy birthday!

小班里的表演
Performing in Kindergarten

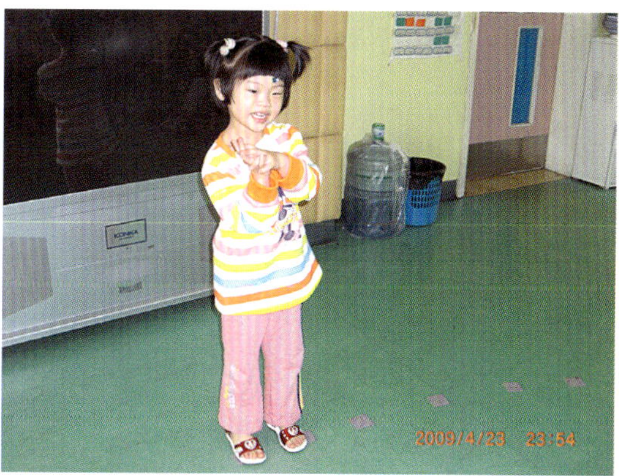

拍拍手 唱歌歌 Clapping Hands, Singing a Song

戴上贝雷帽 How do I look with the beret?

万圣节 Halloween

老师教我叠衣服
Thanks, teacher! I know how to fold clothes now

迎接圣诞节 Christmas is coming!

学认字 How to read...?

我做的环保裙可漂亮啦
My Beautiful "Green" Skirt

环保服装秀 "Green" Fashion Show

“人小鬼大”万圣节趣味造型大比拼

The Award of

Best Make-up & Costume Design

最佳造型奖

Given to 程莲子 for a job well done!

Favorview Palace International Kindergarten

October. 31. 2009

小猫咪 The Little Cat

2008-2009 年第■学期幼儿评价表

姓名：程莲子　　班别：小 企鹅 班　　年龄：3 岁

项目	内容 评价结果
老师的话：	光阴似箭，转眼间又是一个期末的到来了。回首这一学期，莲子在学习、生活等各个方面都有了很大的进步。莲子是个很聪明、很可爱的小女孩，在班上，你的点滴进步老师都看在眼里，乐在心里。看着越来越活泼、越来越出众的莲子，老师在心里祝福：希望这个善良乖巧、惹人疼爱的小宝贝能够永远快乐，天使般的笑容天天出现在这张可爱的小脸蛋上！妹妹很有礼貌，每天一回到幼儿园都会甜甜地叫上一句;老师好。表扬！虽然妹妹有时上课不够认真，但是每次都能很快把老师所教的知识掌握住了。而且本学期妹妹已学会乖乖坐好和其他小朋友一起上课了，希望继续努力！ 莲子妹妹，加油哦！！！
保育老师的话：	莲子小朋友,你是个活泼开朗的小女孩。老师清楚地记得你刚来幼儿园时好多事情都需要老师来帮你,还经常尿裤子。现在的你长大了,每天都会高高兴兴来幼儿园,学会了自己的事情自己做,同伴间能友好相处,活动中能遵守规则。以后如果能大胆地说出自己的想法,就更棒了。
外教的话：Foreign Teacher's comment	Apple adds a lot of character to our classroom. Even though she's usually doing her own thing, she is listening to our class. I often hear her identifying things in English. I even hear her speaking English to herself. I can remember the first two weeks of September when Apple would scream and cry every time she saw me. But now she's my little buddy, and I've grown fond of all her energy. She now can sit nicely with the other students. And she always wants to try any game we play in class.

下学期重点培养或重点关注的方面：

聪明可爱的你本学期又进步了很多，这很好。老师们都很高兴，相信爸爸妈妈也感到欣慰。老师觉得如果你在新的学期里上课更认真，睡觉更乖一点就更棒了！好吗？

血色素：　体重：15.5 公斤　身高：94　评价：中

2008-2009 年第二学期幼儿评价表

姓名：程莲子　　班别：小 企鹅 班　　年龄：4 岁

项目	内容 评价结果
老师的话：	莲子在这个学期进步真的很大！在老师的眼里，你是一个大姐 姐了。在这个学期，莲子开始愿意并投入到学习活动中。在活动中， 莲子会主动举手回答老师的问题，，愿意和同伴分享自己的想法。 接受能力也非常强。但有时喜欢做一些小动作转移注意力，要老师 提醒。莲子很喜欢看书，不过当莲子和小朋友都喜欢一本书时，可 以和小朋友商量哦。自理能力上，每天中午一到起床，莲子能迅速 的自己穿鞋子，自觉的去拿杯子喝水，如果遇到喝酸奶时，莲子就 会特别开心，干任何事情都特别快了，真是个小灵精，哈哈。莲子 这个学期逐渐开始学会和同伴友好相处，还交了一个好朋友：小雅。 希望莲子升班后拥有更多好朋友。祝：暑假愉快！
外教的话：Foreign Teacher's comment	It's such a delight to be Apple's English teacher. She's such a little doll. Things are much different now! In September, she would cry every time I walked into the classroom. Now, she is a very active and enthusiastic member of our class. She enjoys the games and activities we do. Apple also does well and shows great energy when we sing songs and dance. Apple does well when repeating new English words, and is able to repeat new words loudly and clearly. She has been a very energetic participant in our English class. Great work!

下学期重点培养或重点关注的方面：

莲子已经有了那么多的进步，但是如果能不挑食，自己动手吃饭，那就更棒了。努力加油，你会做到的。

血色素：141　体重：16 公斤　身高：97.5　评价：中　乙肝表面抗体：0.48

2010·童话

Fairy Tales

我画“小鱼鱼” I’m drawing “The Little Fish”

鱼儿水里游
花儿土中长
猫儿地上跑
鸟儿天上飞……
家里的墙壁
都是我的画纸
画纸上的图画
都是我的童话……

Swimming is the fish
Smiling are the flowers
Running cats and flying birds
All in my paintings on the walls
Those fairy tales I dreamed
Are like roses in full bloom

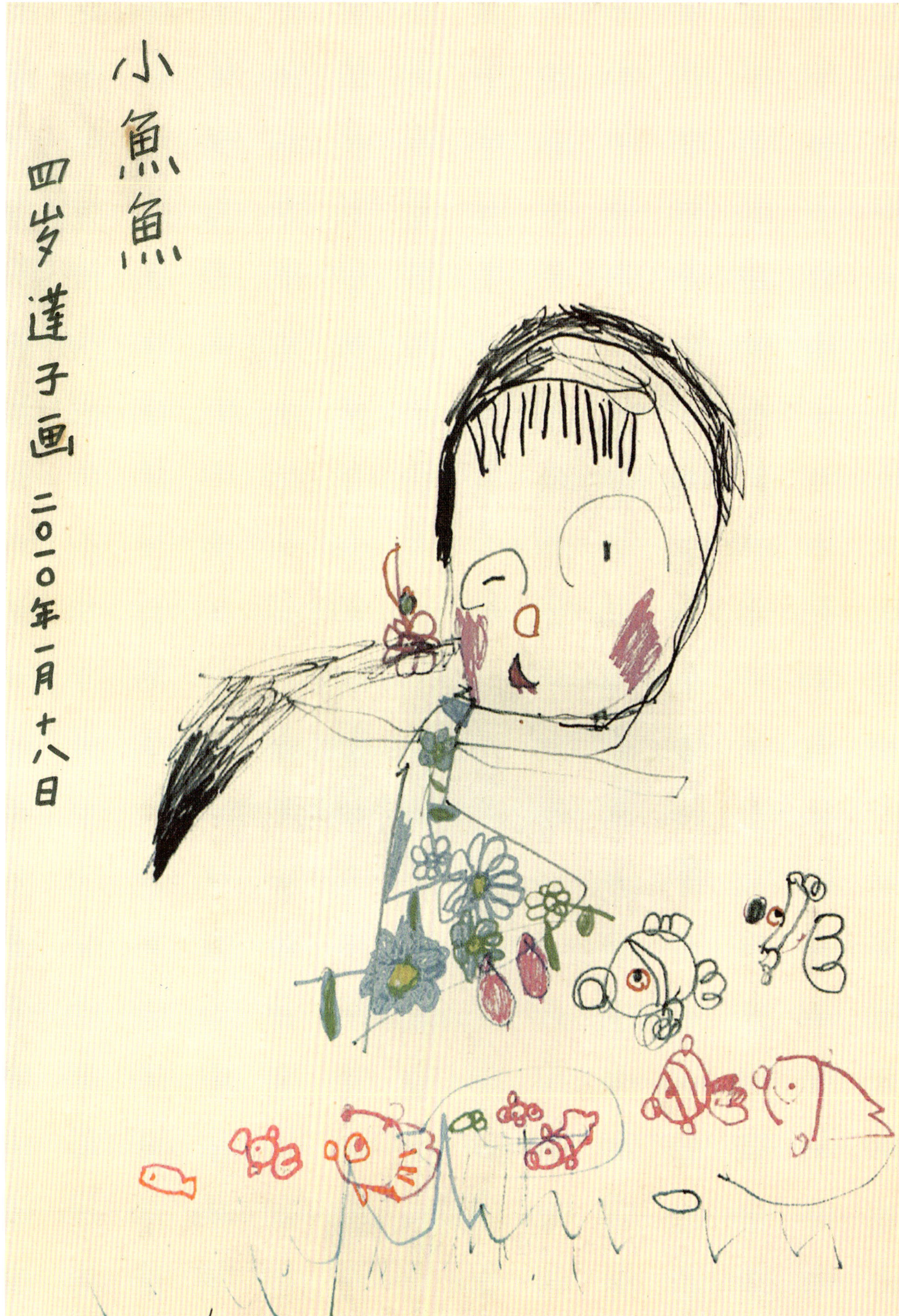

作品点评

扬起的圆脸，整齐的刘海，舒展的双手，甩飞的小辫，都落笔有趣。更妙的是那跃动的身姿和微侧的小嘴，将一个小姑娘追看小鱼时的兴奋神态表现得活灵活现，动感十足。

——张建平

Appreciation of Painting

This picture shows us a lovely girl happily chasing swimming fish. We can see her raised face, tidy bang, stretching arms and flying braid. What's more attractive are her bouncing steps and cute grinning, telling us how excited she is. The girl is portrayed so lifelike that we sometimes believe she is really running in the picture.

—Zhang Jianping

小鱼鱼
The Little Fish

莲子四岁画

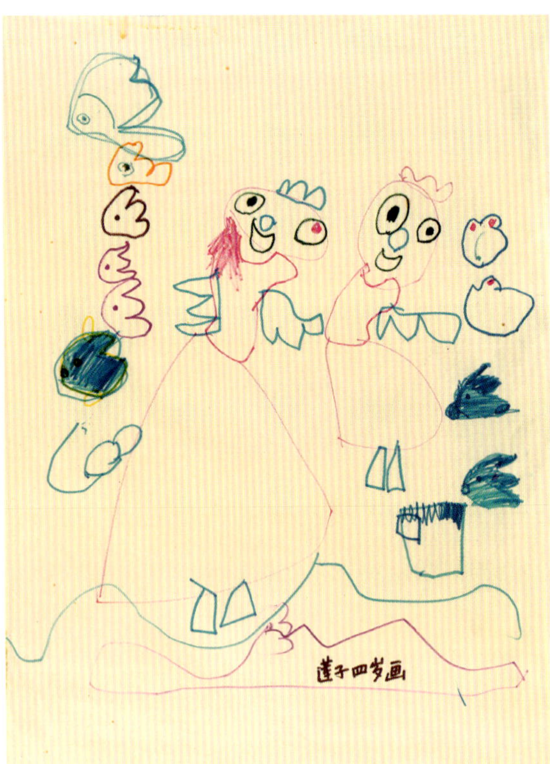

两个小公主 Two Little Princess

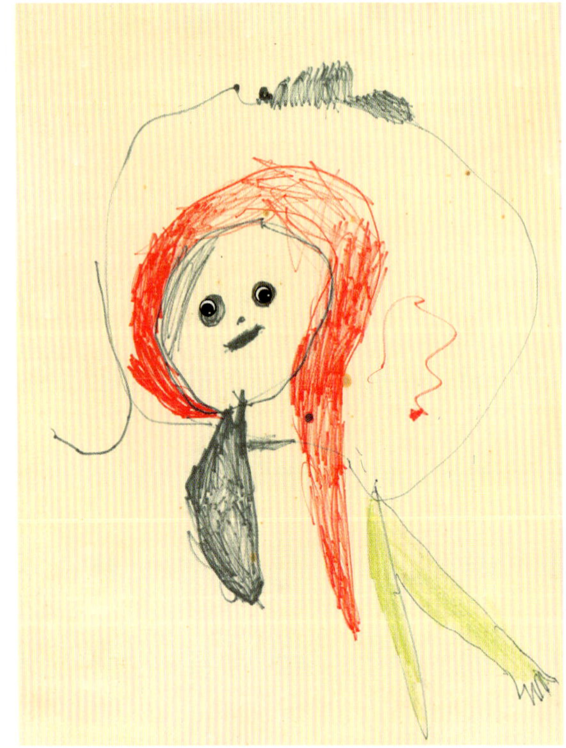

红头发的女孩子真漂亮！
Beautiful Girl with Red Hair

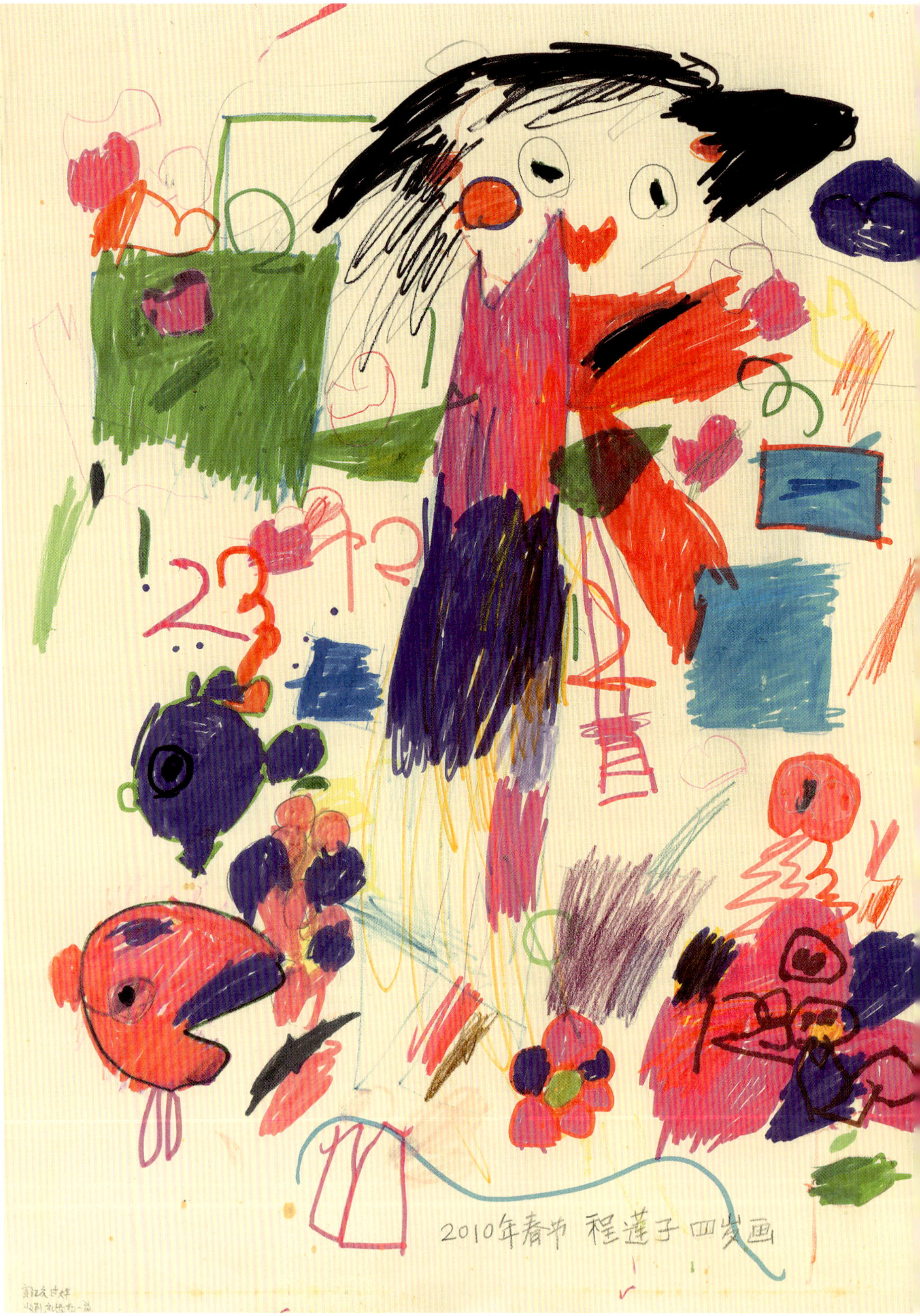
2010年春节 程莲子 四岁画

穿红衣，过新年 Time for New Year, Time for Red

我和家里的苹果树比高高 Who is taller, the apple tree or me?

穿裙子，戴花花 My Fair Lady

戴眼镜的男孩 Ha! Four-Eye Boy

快乐的小女孩 Happy Angel

蓝裙子蓝花花 Blue Skirt and Flowers

小姑娘和蓝裙子　The Little Girl and Blue Dress

天线宝宝　Teletubbies

小女孩和小猫咪　The Little Girl and Little Cat

扎辫子的小姑娘 The Little Girl with Braid

章鱼哥 Mr. Octopus

倒影画 The Reflection Picture

瓢虫 Ladybug

桌子上的花果 Flower and Fruit on the Desk

太阳出，花儿笑 You are my sunshine and I'm your flower

五色大苹果 Big Apple Dyed by the Rainbow

蜗牛 Snail

成长照片

Photos of Different Growth Phases

家涂四壁

The Walls of the House are Full of Paintings

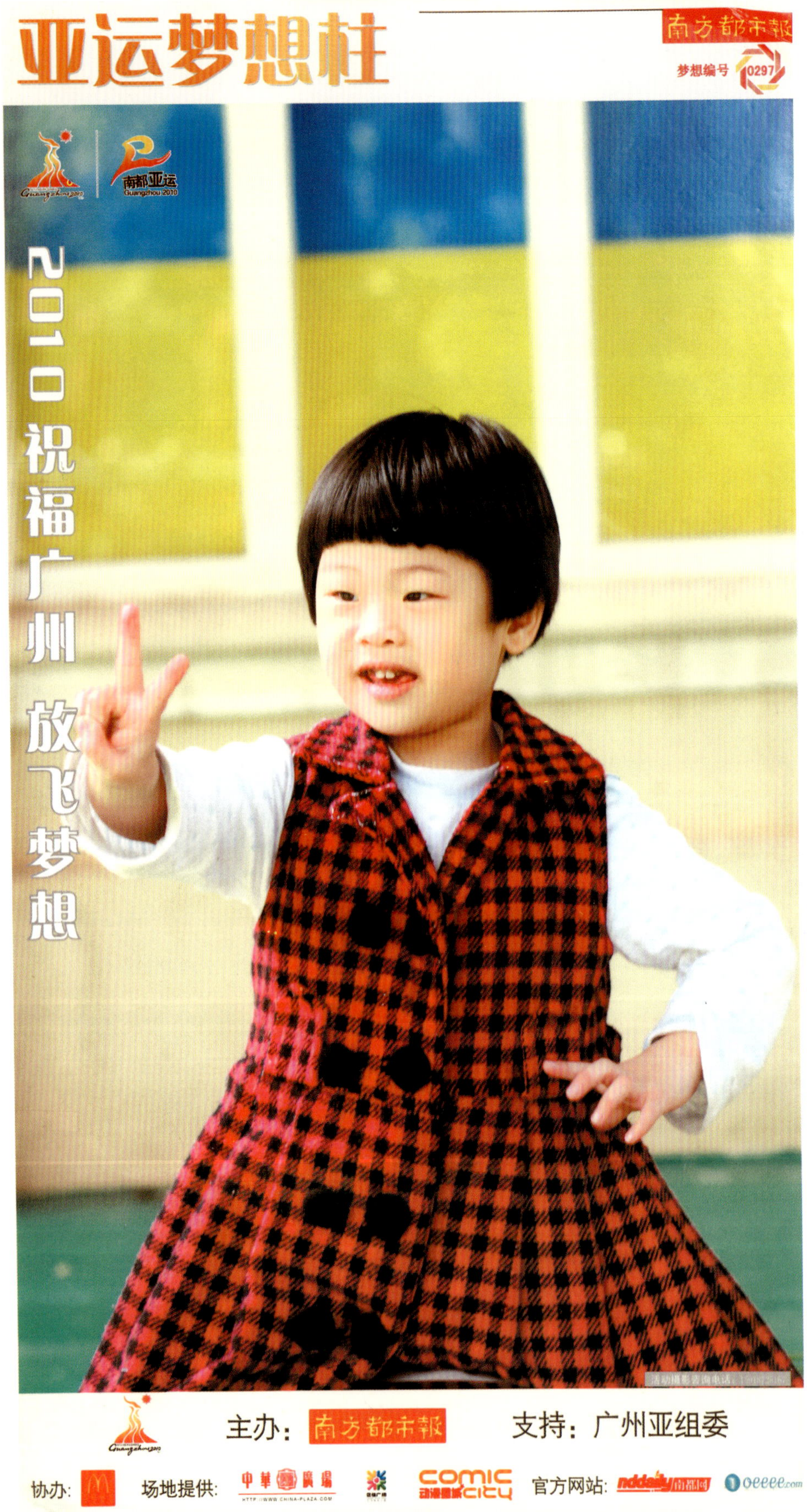

亚运梦想柱

2010祝福广州 放飞梦想

主办：南方都市報 支持：广州亚组委

协办： 场地提供：   官方网站：  

老师说，这些照片是布置在亚运会会场的。耶！

The teacher said these photos would be shown at the venue of the Asian Games. Yeah!

爸爸的画墙 Dad's Painting Wall

摘果果 Picking Fruits

做鬼脸 Making a Face

小兔家 The Rabbit's Home

2009-2010年第一学期幼儿评价表

姓名：程莲子　班别：小兔班　年龄：4岁

项目	内容	评价结果
老师的话：	莲子这个学期升上了小兔班，是大姐姐了，在与人相处方面进步了许多，喜欢能小朋友一起玩游戏，在吃饭方面，挑食方面有了很大的进步哦！这个学期莲子的美术方面进步最明显，还记得刚开学的美术课，莲子只会用蜡笔画简单的图案，颜色也涂不好，现在她能独立作画，能按要求画出事物的大体形态，不需要老师帮忙，并且颜色也涂得非常好。莲子的动手能力也有进步，喜欢操作活动，例如：粘贴，剪纸，装饰等。老师发现莲子的注意力不够集中，在家也可以多让她画画，多做手工方面的活动，可以提高她的做事情的专注力。莲子依然非常喜欢听故事，希望下个学期能大胆讲述给班上小朋友听，好吗？　祝：寒假快乐！	
外教的话：Foreign Teacher's comment	Apple continues to make many great improvements in our class. She is now able to sit nicely during lessons. She is now much more attentive, and is learning to better focus her attention during lessons. Apple often participates in English language games, and is able to complete most tasks. Apple is able to recognize the letters of the alphabet. Apple also has quite a large vocabulary, and often tries to speak to me using the English words she knows. It's so nice to see her improved effort. Way to go!	

下学期重点培养或重点关注的方面：

莲子的自理能力方面还是比较依赖老师的帮助，下个学期午睡要多加油哦！

血色素：148　体重：17kg　身高：101cm　评价：中　口腔保健：正常

2009-2010年第二学期幼儿评价表

姓名：程莲子　班别：小兔班　年龄：5岁

项目	内容	评价结果
老师的话：		下学期我们就要升上大班做大哥哥姐姐了，莲子自从开学以来进步很大，懂事了很多。也变得勇敢了。记得我们开展《蜗牛》方案的时候，莲子很害怕蜗牛，但是经过老师的介绍和小朋友对蜗牛的热情，莲子对小蜗牛也产生了好奇，不害怕了，每天都会去看看小蜗牛长大没有。做实验的时候也敢把头凑前看了。老师看到莲子对学习有这种热情都感到非常高兴。这学期莲子在吃饭方面也进步了，虽然有时还是要老师喂，但是很多时候莲子可以坚持把饭菜独立吃完，中午莲子虽然睡不着，但是她知道不影响其他小朋友，会在床上安静躺着或问老师可不可以到教室玩玩具。老师相信莲子以后会有更多让老师表扬的优点的，继续加油！ 祝：暑假愉快！
外教的话： Foreign Teacher's comment		Apple has made many great improvements this semester. She is now much more adjusted to our class dynamic, and has been a more active participant. Apple is learning to listen more carefully during lessons and to follow directions in English. Apple shows interest to participate in the songs, games and activities we do in English class. It has been wonderful to see Apple become such an active participant in our class. Great work! Have a nice summer!

下学期重点培养或重点关注的方面：

莲子这个学期回幼儿园的时间比较少，错过了很多有趣的事，希望莲子多吃饭，多锻炼，下学期多多参加幼儿园活动哦！

2011 · 童趣

Interesting Memories

跟着爸爸去写生　Go Drawing from Nature with Dad

美丽景色的写生
开阔了我想象的空间
从小爱读的童话故事
变成了我笔下的图画

Beautiful scenery that we sketched
Opens the door to boundless world of imagination
The fairy tales I loved as a little girl
Are now becoming vivid under my brush

阳光女孩　Sunshine Girls

小公主和大红花　Little Princess and Big Red Flower

猜猜三个姑娘想什么？　What do they want? Can you guess?

可爱小公主　The Lovely Little Princess

小姑娘采花花　Little Girl Picking Flowers

跳舞的女孩　Dancing Girls

摸摸妈妈肚里的小宝宝 Hello, do you hear me?

魔法师来啦！ The magician is coming!

米奇和米妮 Mickey and Minnie

孙悟空抢金宝葫芦 I'm Monkey King. Give me the Gold Cucurbit!

阳光下的小姑娘　Little Girls in the Sunshine

采花花　Picking Flowers

热闹的海底　What a party under the Sea!

美人鱼看鱼鱼　Mermaid:" Fish... I'm fish, too!"

花裙子　Floral Dress

房子、大树和花花　Dream House with a Large Tree and Flowers

门口开着鲜花　Flowers prefer to stay out

我在花园捉迷藏　Hide-and-Seek in the Garden

树上开满红花　A Melody Tree

月光下的池塘　The Pond in the Moonlight

彩色的小屋子　Colorful Cottage

阳光下的车车　A car in the Sunshine

红绿灯 Traffic Lights

鳄鱼 Crocodile

坐马车 By Carriage

圣诞贺卡　Christmas Card

Photos of Different Growth Phases

表演 Performing

三亚：看海、踏浪、捡贝壳
Sanya: Watching the Sea, Stepping the Waves and Collecting Shells

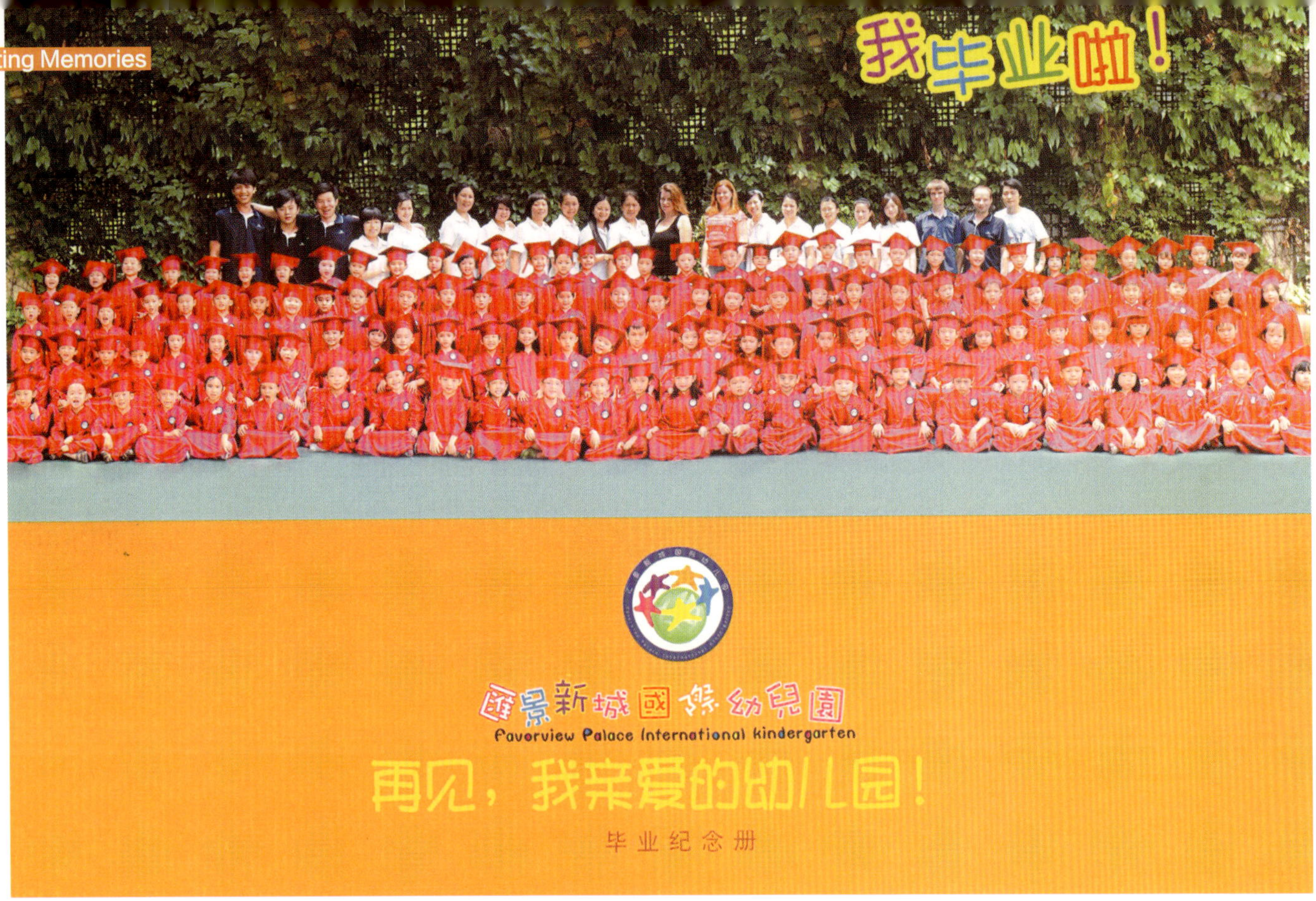

我毕业啦！

匯景新城國際幼兒園
Favorview Palace International kindergarten

再见，我亲爱的幼儿园！

毕业纪念册

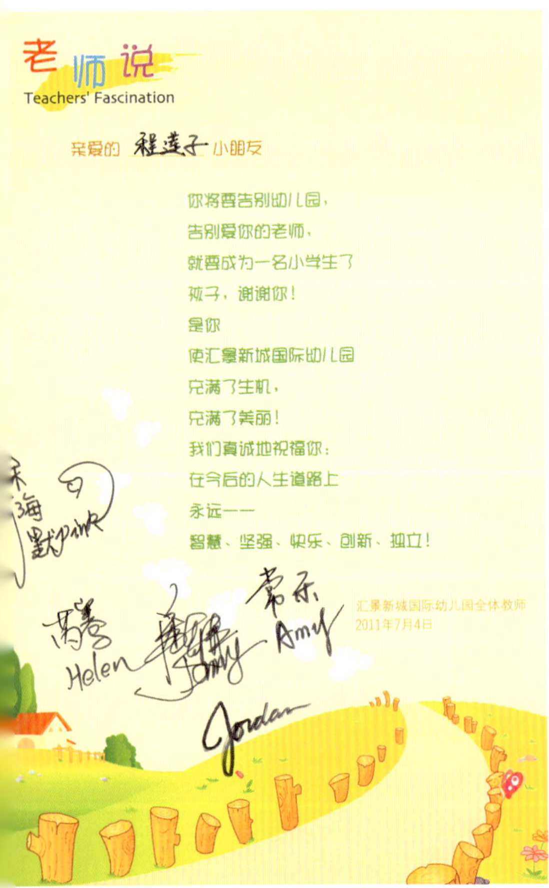

老师说
Teachers' Fascination

亲爱的 程逵子 小朋友

你将要告别幼儿园，
告别爱你的老师，
就要成为一名小学生了
孩子，谢谢你！
是你
使汇景新城国际幼儿园
充满了生机，
充满了美丽！
我们真诚地祝福你：
在今后的人生道路上
永远——
智慧、坚强、快乐、创新、独立！

汇景新城国际幼儿园全体教师
2011年7月4日

我的 班毕业合影

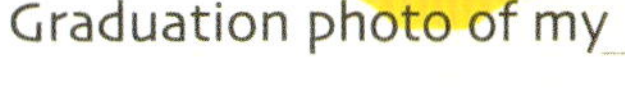

Graduation photo of my ________ class

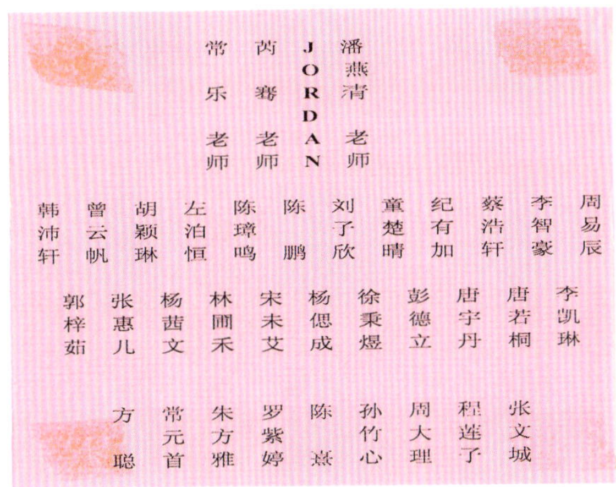

潘燕清老师　JORDAN　芮骞老师　常乐老师

周易辰　李智豪　蔡浩轩　纪有加　童楚晴　刘子欣　陈鹏　陈璋鸣　左泊恒　胡颖琳　曾云帆　韩沛轩

李凯琳　唐若桐　唐宇丹　彭德立　徐秉煜　杨偲成　宋未艾　林圃禾　杨茜文　张蕙儿　郭梓茹

张文城　程莲子　周大理　孙竹心　陈熹　罗紫婷　朱方雅　常元首　方聪

FAVORVIEW PALACE INTERNATIONAL KINDERGARTEN

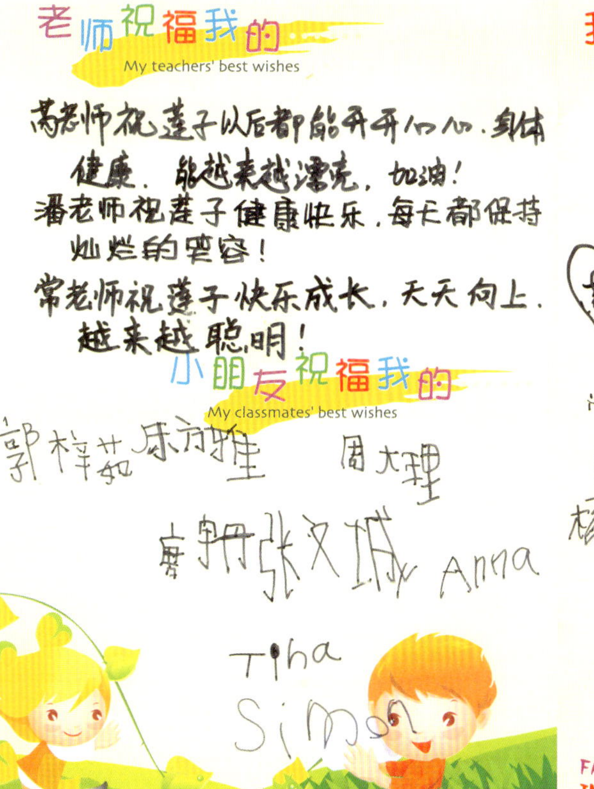

幼儿园毕业证书
Graduation Certificate of Kindergarten

汇景新城国际幼儿园

2010-2011 学年第一学期幼儿评价表

姓名：程莲子　班别：小鹿班　年龄：6 岁

项目	内容 评价结果
生长发育	缺勤没有体检
老师的话：	本学期莲子升上了大班，是幼儿园最大的姐姐了，虽然请假两星期去了北京，在幼儿园的时间不多，但莲子各方面都有了很大的进步，早上来园能有礼貌的向老师问好，很棒哦！ 还记得小兔班的时候，莲子吃饭还需要老师喂，但到了大班以后基本能自己进餐，以前不爱吃青菜的她，现在每顿饭都能吃幼儿园煮的青菜。起床以后能自己穿衣服和鞋子，而且动作比较快，偶尔还会穿翻鞋子，但老师一提醒能马上换过来。在美术方面，老师发现莲子的画也有了很大的进步，画面比以前的要更丰富，有层次，并且色彩搭配也很特别，有自己的想法，作品能出人意料。这个学期她还参加了全脑数学的兴趣班，聪明的她能很快掌握题型，并专注和认真的完成操作练习，作业干净整洁，数字书写也非常好看，但是要注意画画和做练习的时候头要抬高点哦！莲子还很喜欢表演，在这次的圣诞活动中，莲子能和小朋友一起在台上跟着音乐的节奏又唱又跳呢！ 在与人交往方面，莲子也有了进步，她能主动与小朋友交往，与人分享自己喜欢的东西，相信这样她的在班上的好朋友会越来越多，但是老师发现莲子的依赖性还是比较强，有时候喜欢依赖老师的帮助，希望莲子能尽快的独立起来。下个学期是幼小衔接的时候，莲子不要再请那么长的假哦！ 祝：寒假快乐！预祝春节快乐，身体健康！
外教的话：Foreign Teacher's comment	Apple has done very well this semester. She has such a friendly and positive personality that we all appreciate. She is always smiling and seems to really enjoy our class. It's great to see that Apple really enjoys learning English. She always gives her best effort. Apple is able to express herself using simple English sentences. She repeats new words well, and is a very active member of our class. Great work! Happy New Year!
下学期重点培养或重点关注的方面： 希望莲子下学期早上能早点回园参加早锻活动，这样可以帮助中午的入睡，对以后去小学会有很大的帮助哦！	

汇景新城国际幼儿园

FAVORVIEW PALACE INTERNATIONAL KINDERGARTEN

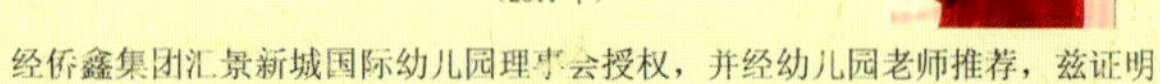

毕业证书

（2011 年）

经侨鑫集团汇景新城国际幼儿园理事会授权，并经幼儿园老师推荐，兹证明：

程莲子

已出色完成了在本园幼儿教育课程的学习，特颁此证。

二零一一年七月九日

杨渊

汇景新城国际幼儿园园长
Angel Yang
Principal of Favorview Palace International Kindergarten

FAVORVIEW PALACE INTERNATIONAL KINDERGARTEN

Certificate of Graduation

(Class of 2011)

By Authority of the Board of Trustees of

Favorview Palace International Kindergarten

(A Member of the Education Division of Kingold Group)

And upon recommendation of the Kindergarten of the Staff

Apple

Has been admitted to having successfully completed the requirement of the program with outstanding achievement.

Witness of the seal of the Favorview Palace International Kindergarten and the signatures of its Off

This ninth day of July, two thousand and eleven

做有中国灵魂有世界眼光的人

2

节目名称：逐梦

表演形式：歌舞

演　　员：一年级女生

指导老师：叶彬

艺术特色：

与成人舞蹈相比，少儿舞蹈的律动更为欢快明朗，它包容少儿的“童心”与“童趣”，孩子们通过舞蹈的具体形象来认识缤纷的世界，认识真善美，从而培养她们感受美、欣赏美、追求美的能力，还能增强身体协调性，培养良好的节奏感。

我自己选择 我才会负责

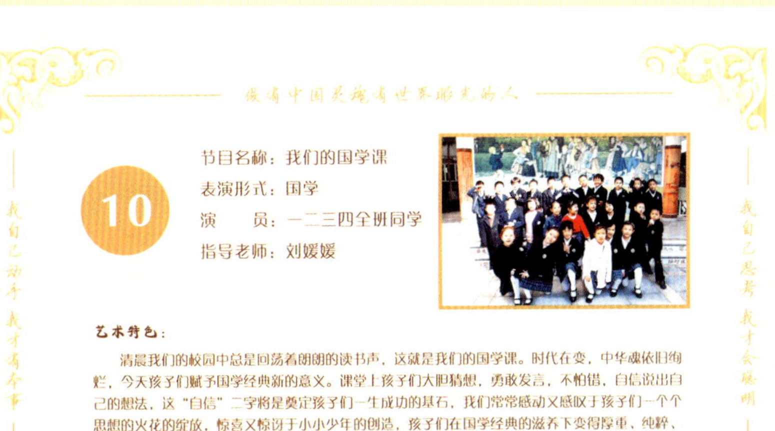

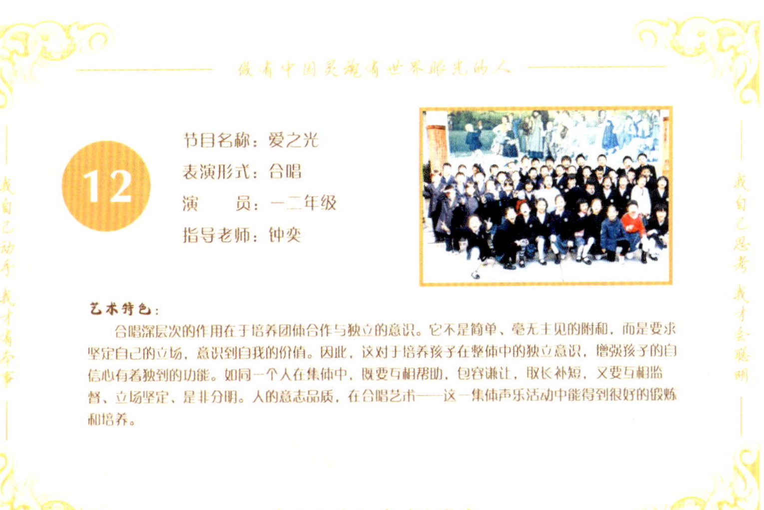

参加小学五周年庆典　Attending the Fifth Anniversary of My Primary School

问候卡

我刚入读小学一年级时，在学校参加户外活动不小心受伤不能回学校上课，老师给我带来班上 20 多个同学写下的关心问候卡，我很感动！

Greeting card

When I was in grade one, I got injured while taking part in outdoor activities at school. I couldn't go to school for a while. One day the teacher brought me a card with the greetings of more than 20 of my classmates. I was deeply moved!

莲子
我 xiān
说 zhù 你
早日 kāng fù
rán hòu
zhù 你 xīn
年 lè. shēng
tǐ jiàn kāng
xiè xiè

祝 莲子
早日康复!

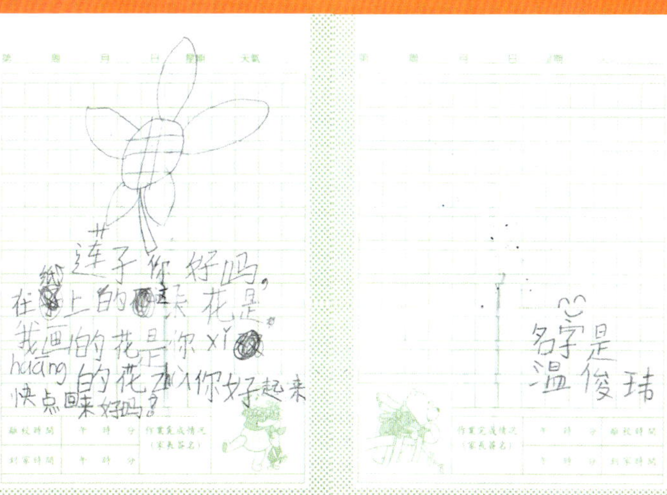
名字是
温俊玮

2012 · 向往

Longings

2012 年 8 月广东美术馆，爸爸的画展开幕式，林墉舅爷爷（左三）拉着我的手很开心

In August, 2008, at dad's art exhibition opening at Guangdong Museums of Art, granduncle Lin Yong(third from left) was holding my hand happily

2012 年 12 月北京中国美术馆展览大厅，爸爸的画展开幕式，大厅摆着爸爸和我的画

In December, 2008, at dad's art exhibition opening at National Art Museum of China in Beijing, both dad's and my paintings were displayed in the hall

爸爸的画展
从广东到北京中国美术馆
我的画作
也从广州到了北京
走进五彩缤纷的艺术殿堂
追逐快乐无限的艺术梦想

Daddy's art exhibitions
From Guangdong to National Art Museum of China in Beijing
My paintings
Just followed my daddy's heel
Entering the artistic paradise
To chase a infinite dream of art

变色花
Color-Changing Flower

紫罗兰花园　Violet Garden

山上的亭子 The Pavilion on the Hill

山中小屋 The House on the Hill

我和妈妈在山上 Mom and I on the Hill

山中温泉　Spring in the Mountain

坐车车　Go For a Ride

海底世界 The Undersea World

森林里的小屋子 The House in the Forest

彩虹下的荷塘 The Pond Under the Rainbow

童话故事里的公主们 Princesses in Fairy Tales

小鱼儿，您好！ Hello, Fish!

红头发的美人鱼 The Mermaid with Red Hair

小美人鱼、比目鱼和水母
Little Mermaid, Flounder and Jellyfish

美人鱼带着小水母参观海底世界
Mermaid: Little Jellyfish, welcome to the undersea world. I'm your tour guide

小姑娘和向日葵　The Little Girl and Sunflower

小公主和荷花　Little Princess and Lotus

小公主　The Little Princess

黄裙子，绿裙子　Yellow Skirt and Green Skirt

嫦娥飞月宫 Chang'e Flying to the Moon

简单的生活 Simple Life

神话中的三头孔雀
Three-Head Peacock in Myth

林黛玉与薛宝钗 Lin Daiyu and Xue Baochai

作品点评

这幅《祝爸爸画展成功》的画，初看朴朴素素的画面，表达了小女孩给爸爸的祝福。但细细观看，却发现在祝贺的主题下，隐藏着小画家对事物超乎年龄的认知和思想：一幢写着“中国美术馆”的楼画得高大巍峨，表示这里是中国最高的艺术殿堂；前面的荷花绿叶，是爸爸画展主题《荷语》的形象表现；升腾的彩色气球中，有一个是心的形状，那是不是要表达对爸爸画展发自内心的祝贺？而那个高高的阶梯，更是耐人寻味地表现了：进入中国美术馆展览是一件非常不容易的事，需要努力攀登、攀登……画面没有多余的笔墨，每处的着笔，都蕴含着非同寻常的寓意！令人不由得赞叹的是，这是一个仅七岁小女孩的作品！

——张建平

Appreciation of Painting

This picture may seem plain at first sight. But it conveys the little girl's best wishes for her dear father. When we settle down to savor it, we will discover that, under the cover of congratulations, the little painter concealed such mellow understanding of things that is rarely seen in a little child at her age. Look, the building in the picture is named “National Art Museum of China”. Our painter gave it a majestic look which rightly symbolizes its supreme status in China as the top palace of art; Moving our eyes downward to find the lotuses in delicate red and their verdant leaves, apparently, they echo with the father's art exhibition—Lotus Talk; Up to the top, a row of brightly colored balloons fly into our sights. See the heart-shaped one? Isn't it the daughter's heart-felt wish for her father? While the towering stair may be even more thought-provoking. The painter seems to tell us how arduous it is to enter the National Art Museum of China. To get there, one must climb up step by step...Without a single redundancy, every touch of the paintbrush on the paper was meant to express special meaning. Can you believe the painter is only seven-year-old?

—Zhang Jianping

祝爸爸画展成功

Wish My Dad a Successful Exhibition

南瓜灯　Pumpkin Light

花果　Flowers and Fruits

终极龙神　The Super Dragon

蓝色的花　Blue Flower

水母　Jellyfish

参加广东美术馆爸爸的个人画展，林墉舅爷爷抱着我
At dad' s art exhibition at Guangdong Museum of Art, granduncle Lin Yong was holding me

爸爸个人画展的开幕式，七岁的我是最小的列席代表
At the opening of dad' s art exhibition, I was the youngest guest

参加北京中国美术馆爸爸的个人画展，
我负责接待和摄影

At dad's art exhibition at National Art Museum of China in Beijing, I was the little receptionist and photographer

三亚：海边跳舞、堆沙　Sanya: Dancing on the Beach, Playing with the Sand

我的小肚兜　My Little Apron

花田 The Sea of Flower

放风筝 Flying Kite

看，我很神气！ Look, I'm so smart!

钢琴秀 Piano Show

上网 Surfing the Internet

老师评价 Teacher's Comments

（一年级上学期）

在数学这门学科里，你学得最得意是图形的认识，不管什么图形，不管它怎样摆放，你都能够一眼识破它。

——数学老师 Math

莲子是个热爱大自然的孩子，你喜欢学校里鸡蛋花树上掉下来的花和叶子，你喜欢画画……还记得你跟我说你去抓小螃蟹的事情吗？好喜欢听你讲述这些有趣的事情！你这个聪明的小家伙，当我还在为你的听课效率大伤脑筋的时候，你却丝毫不差地掌握了所学知识，让我虚惊了一场！

——英语老师 English

在科学课上，你喜欢从与众不同的角度去思考，十分的积极踊跃，观点独特，总能想到别人想不到的方法。记得有一次，你侃侃而谈，声音嘹亮清晰地介绍你的想法，让老师和其他同学都很佩服，期待你以后继续给我们带来惊喜！

——科学老师 Science

你是个可爱的小女孩，总是带着一副天真无邪的笑容。看你的画面总能让我看到惊奇的色彩，看到你心中的童话故事。

——美术老师 Art

你，活泼可爱，性格鲜明，很有自己的想法，并能大胆表达出来。下棋是一项需要静心的活动，愿你能沉静下来，细细品味内里的乐趣。

——围棋老师 Chess

音乐、舞蹈课上你的感受力和表现力不由得让人侧目。

——舞武老师 Dance and Kongfu

莲子，还记得我们刚见面的时候吗？你拒绝我的接近，总是低垂着眼帘，把自己扮演成一个小 baby。后来，我发现你有着极好的记忆力，有着极高的绘画天分，还有着极浓厚的读书欲望，这样的你怎么可能像你表现出来的那么娇弱？于是，我和妈妈一起下定决心，改变了对你的态度，也许这段日子你会感到委屈，怎么原来无条件包容你的两个人一下子这么严厉？是不是不爱你了？宝贝，我们对你的爱仍和从前一样，没少半分，只是，我们要换一种方式，换一种可以让你从小 baby 变成一个真正的小学生，一个真正快乐的有朋友、有本事的女孩子的方式。你没有让我们失望。随着你对校园生活的越来越熟悉，你开朗了，和同学们有说有笑，你认真了，课文读得有声有色，你的眼睛抬起来直视着我了，让我走进了你的世界，这一切是我们共同努力的结果。

——班主任老师 Master teacher

在宿舍里，你学会了自己穿衣、刷牙、梳头发；学着自己叠衣服、叠被子，都做得有模有样。看着逐渐进步的你，老师真以你为傲。

——生活老师 Nursing Teacher

爸爸妈妈对你说 Parent's Comment

宝贝，你不到 6 岁妈妈就将你送进了学校，在家里人的一片反对声中，妈妈怀着忐忑不安的心情，抱着你的衣服把你留在学校寄宿。记得 9 月 6 日那天上午，就是妈妈要出国的前一天，忽然心里特别不安特别想看看你，于是妈妈给老师打了电话，下午早早就赶回家，等啊等，最终等到天黑了，妈妈都没能见到你。那天晚上，妈妈躺在卧室的摇椅眼泪不停地流，吃不下一口饭。第二天 7:30，妈妈让司机开车绕到你学校门口，怀着从未有过的离别的不安上了飞机。9 月 9 日晚上，妈妈远在国外接到外婆的电话，说你的脚受伤了，很肿，还重感冒，“莲子说，昨晚脚痛到睡不着，所以感冒了。”第二天一早，外婆又给妈妈打电话，说她整晚没睡，睡不着。刹那间，妈妈的心真的好痛！每当老师向妈妈反映你在学校的问题；或者，你在学校觉得受了委屈回来跟妈妈诉说；还有，那次公开周，妈妈亲眼看到有个高年级的女生走到正在排队跳绳的你后面“啪”“啪”两下打在你的脸，你害怕地躲闪着不敢吭一声……妈妈就会在心里反问自己：是不是真的不应该让你这么小就独自去面对外面的世界？

第一学期过去了，妈妈看到老师们对你的评价，不安之余稍有了一些安慰。孩子，妈妈知道你一路走来不容易，但你坚持了。虽然前面的路依然坑坑洼洼，虽然妈妈不再牵着你的小手在旁边守护着你，但妈妈的心，永远都在你前行的路上陪伴着你。孩子，不管前面的日子是阳光灿烂还是刮风下雨，我们都要勇敢地走下去！

摘自《汇景新城实验小学学生素质发展评价表》

老师评价 Teacher's Comments

（一年级下学期）

莲子，其实你有学好数学的能力，但你却不好好学它，每当写作业的时候，要么你用“我不会”来推卸自己的责任，要么就嘟着小嘴开始生气，真让我替你担心。其实当你用心写字的时候，数字写得相当漂亮、工整；当你用心读书的时候，声音是那么的甜美；有了成就感后，下课还会主动找我玩游戏，只是这样给我们彼此相互了解的机会还是太少了。孩子，人总是要长大的，真心希望你快快长大！

——数学老师 Math

There are some days when you are such a great student to have in class. You know how to sit nicely and do your work very carefully. I remember one class you were the first student to finish your writing and it was done very neatly and organized. We played a game that class where the teacher asked you to write an English word on the blackboard and you were the first one to finish and sit down. The students were very proud of you' and everyone clapped. You were so happy, do you remember?

——英语老师 English

小小的你有一颗细腻敏锐的心，善于捕捉无处不在的美，一声鸟啼一朵落花，都能引起你的注意，使你容易沉浸在自己的世界中。课堂上，你也有自己的见解，在语言表达方面有很强的优势，特别让人惊叹的是，你认识的字很多，一段文章交给你，除了个别生字，你都能流利地读完。表演起来举手投足也一板一眼。

——选修课老师 Elective Course

莲子在艺术方面的悟性如同她的画，在平淡的世界里给人一抹清新，一份惊喜，只是课堂上的规则是要遵守的，不能随心所欲，把你的激情，你的张扬在思想的领域尽情畅享吧。

——选修课老师 Elective Course

还记得你刚刚打算和我做朋友时，经常用你特有的方式和我打招呼，每当想起当初的那一声声“老先生”都会让我不由地笑染眉梢，也许若干年后再回想这一幕，我们彼此都仍能记得。“六一”活动时你的表演更是精彩，那个穿着戏装的小小女孩多像一朵清新的荷花啊！让大家为你送上了热烈掌声的还不仅仅是那漂亮的扮相，还有你的自信，你的大方，那比什么都珍贵！就这样，你一点一点地变化着，你知道吗，现在的你有着很美很美的笑容，而有笑容的女孩是能够得到更多幸运的。

——班主任老师 Master Teacher

善良、单纯的你，每天都是第一个来摆好碗筷，然后，高高兴兴地跑到餐厅外面等待家族成员来吃饭，一个一个地接进来。你不挑食，什么菜都吃一些，吃饭越来越专心了，最近几个周，几乎没有因为吃饭慢而迟回教室了。为此，你很开心，走的时候都会骄傲地告诉老师：“我吃完了！”然后就开心回到班上读书。你一直住在一楼女生宿舍，与家族分开，现在你主动要回二楼宿舍和家族人一起住，甭提大家多高兴了！欢迎你！可爱的孩子！

——生活老师 Nursing Teacher

爸爸妈妈对你说 Parent's Comment

宝贝，不管你长到多少岁，你永远是爸爸、妈妈心中的最爱！一年的学习终于在酷热的夏天结束了，爸爸、妈妈在充满担心与期待中看到了你的成长！成长的你，展现给我们的是越来越有礼貌、有爱心的女儿，在妈妈生病的这个漫长的暑假，你虽然很渴望与其他小朋友那样到处去玩，但你却选择守候在妈妈身边，你坚持说：“妈妈生病了，我要留在家里照顾妈妈。”生活当中你经常有许许多多举动令我们感动；成长的你，更加懂事而明白道理，你能够冷静聆听我们的教育，接受我们的意见，开始学习像大人那样跟我们沟通；成长的你，独立意识越来越强，常常自告奋勇承担生活事务。但面对并不多的作业你却缺乏足够的耐心，任由自己的兴趣更加多地选择自己喜爱的书、画学习。妈妈想方设法寻找更多的道理与你沟通，过程艰难而漫长。宝贝，希望你能够尽快调整自己，成长为全面发展的好孩子。

摘自《汇景新城实验小学学生素质发展评价表》

奖状

慎思·笃学　厚德·博雅

程莲子

在 2011—2012学年第一学期 中，表现突出，成绩优秀，荣获 善于发现 奖。

特发此状，以资鼓励！

匯景新城實驗小學
Favorview Palace Primary School
2012年1月12日

奖状

慎思·笃学　厚德·博雅

程莲子

在 2011-2012学年下学期 中，表现突出，成绩优秀，荣获 戏苑小莲花 奖。

特发此状，以资鼓励！

匯景新城實驗小學
Favorview Palace Primary School
2012年7月8日

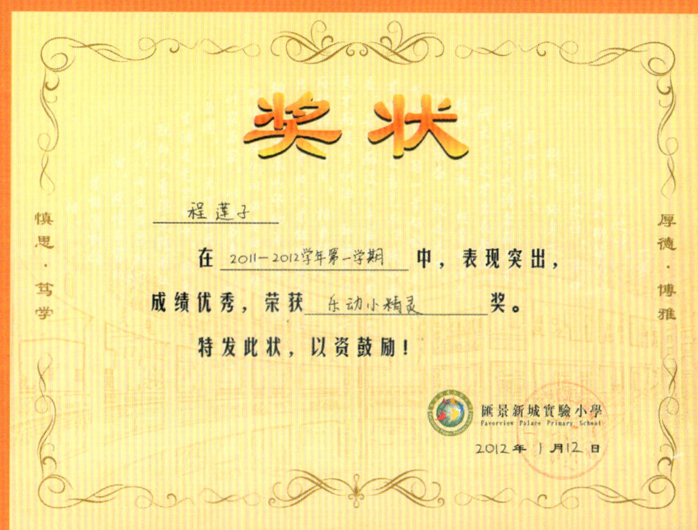

奖状

慎思·笃学　厚德·博雅

程莲子

在 2011—2012学年第一学期 中，表现突出，成绩优秀，荣获 乐动小精灵 奖。

特发此状，以资鼓励！

匯景新城實驗小學
Favorview Palace Primary School
2012年1月12日

奖状

慎思·笃学　厚德·博雅

程莲子

在 2011-2012学年下学期 中，表现突出，成绩优秀，荣获 英语规范书写 奖。

特发此状，以资鼓励！

匯景新城實驗小學
Favorview Palace Primary School
2012年7月8日

奖状

慎思·笃学　厚德·博雅

程莲子

在 2011—2012学年第一学期 中，表现突出，成绩优秀，荣获 快乐小女生 奖。

特发此状，以资鼓励！

匯景新城實驗小學
Favorview Palace Primary School
2012年1月12日

奖状

慎思·笃学　厚德·博雅

程莲子

在 2011-2012学年下学期 中，表现突出，成绩优秀，荣获 童话故事大王 奖。

特发此状，以资鼓励！

匯景新城實驗小學
Favorview Palace Primary School
2012年7月8日

2013 · 学海

Sea of learning

在新加坡海洋馆 Aquarium in Singapore

我像乘上了学海的一叶小舟
在学校，老师是舵手
在家里，舵手是爸爸妈妈
而我，始终是快乐的小水手

I take a little boat
Floating on the sea of learning
My teachers are the helmsman
When my boat drifting to school
My dad and mom are the steersman
When the boat drifting home
And as always
I am the little jolly sailor

水仙花　Daffodils

扇画：向日葵　Fan Painting : Sunflowers

竹子　Bamboo

南瓜比赛　Pumpkin Contest

螃蟹岛　Crab Island

彩虹鸡　Rainbow Chicken

蝴蝶王国　Butterfly Kingdom

水母和美人鱼　Jellyfish and Mermaid

线画 Line Drawing

鸭子、美人鱼和小树　Duck、Mermaid and Tree

广州少儿公园　Guangzhou Children's Park

森林　Forest

池塘　Pond

这是春天，这是小河　Miss Spring and Mr.River

动漫美人鱼　Cartoon Mermaid

七彩美人鱼　Colorful Mermaid

小美人鱼　The Little Mermaid

最美的衣服　The Most Beautiful Clothes

芭比娃娃 Barbie

芭比公主和小狗 Barbie and Little Dog

芭比之服 Barbie's Costumes

问你怎么设计？ How do you design？

奇妙的国度 Wonderful Kingdom

白蛇与青蛇 The White Snake and the Green Snake

女豪杰 Heroine

西施浣纱 Xishi washing clothes

嫦娥奔月 Chang'e Flying to the Moon

美少女　Beautiful Little Girl

动漫少女　Cartoon Girl

清远小公主　Qingyuan Little Princess

光头强的秘密计划　Bald Qiang's Secretive Plan

跳皮筋 Jumping Rubber Band

年轻的妈妈和帅气的爸爸 A Perfect Match!-My Mom and Dad

祝爸爸早日健康 Wish Dad Good Health

沙漠上的小姑娘 Little Girl in the Desert

游泳池 Swimming Pool

中国古代四大名著人物
Figures in China's Four Ancient Novels

哪吒与王母娘娘 Ne Zha and Mother Wang

林黛玉与贾宝玉 Lin Daiyu and Jia Baoyu

《三国演义》人物 Figures in *Romance of the Three Kingdoms*

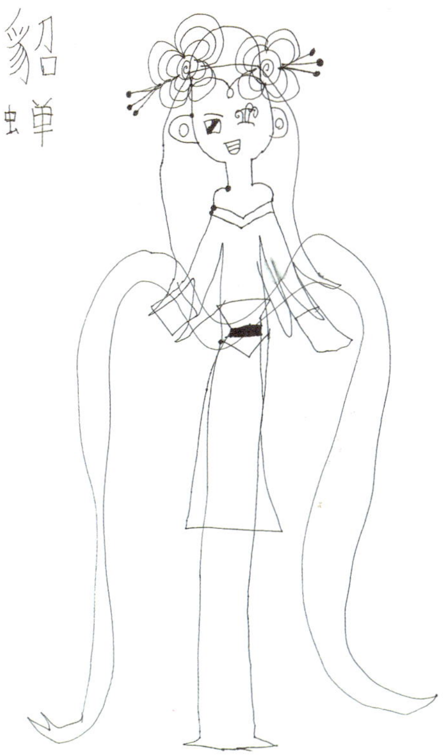

貂蝉

貂蝉　Diaochan

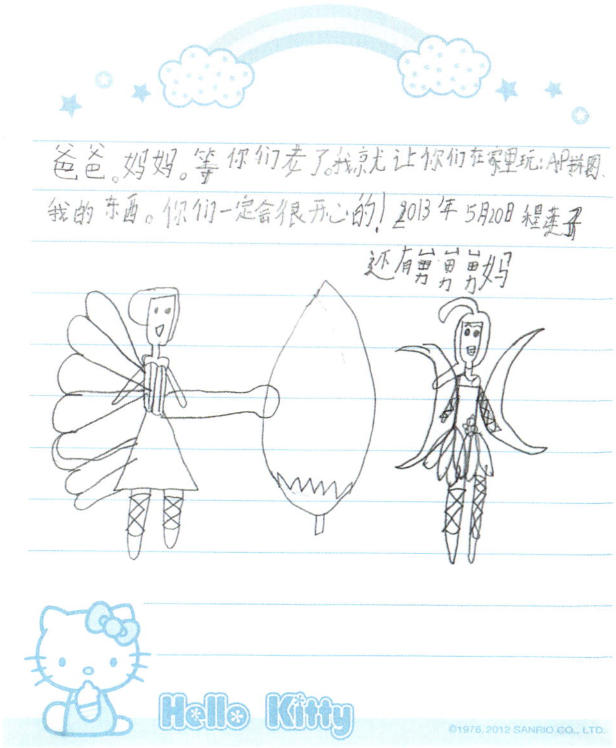

爸爸、妈妈。等你们老了，我就让你们在家里玩：AP游戏。我的东西。你们一定会很开心的！2013年5月20日 程建开

还有舅舅舅妈

写给爸爸妈妈的话　Letter to Mom and Dad

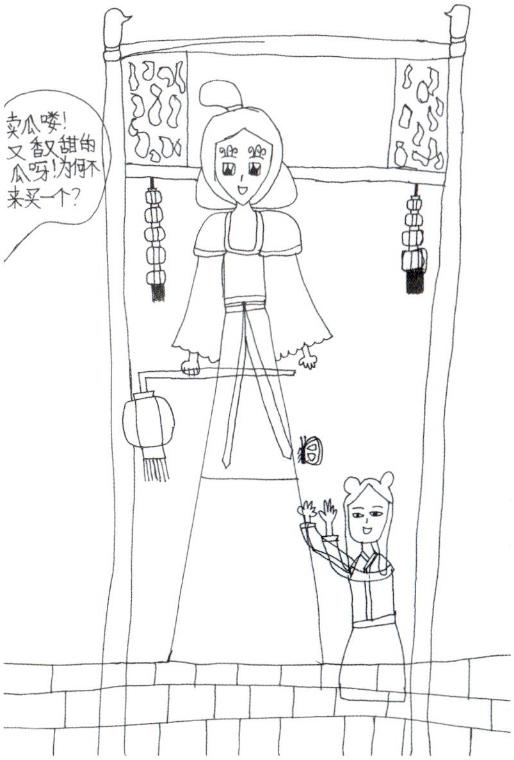

卖瓜喽！又甜又甜的瓜呀！为何不来买一个？

卖瓜姑娘　A Girl Selling Mellon

美好的世界　Beautiful World

赛尔号精灵宝典　The Fairy Book of Saier

摄影作品

Photography Works

三亚风光 Picturesque Scenery in Sanya

苏州园林　Gardens in Suzhou

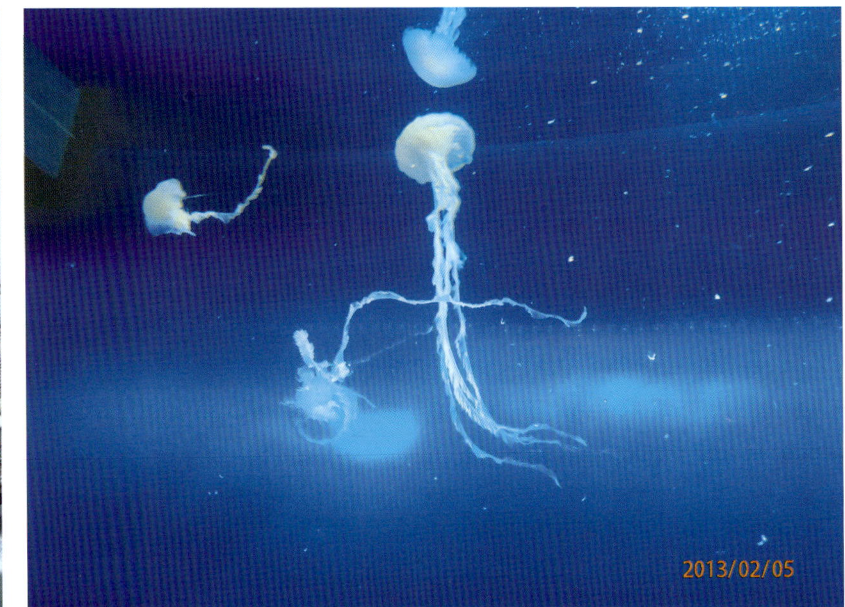

新加坡
Singapore

新加坡旅游

Trip in Singapore

北京格格秀
Many Styles of Princesses (Beijing)

北京格格秀

Many Styles of Princesses (Beijing)

赈灾义演　Charity Performance

爸爸教我画画　You draw, I draw

我喜欢亲妈妈　Mom, how about one more kiss?

享受三亚的阳光
Enjoying the Sunshine in Sanya

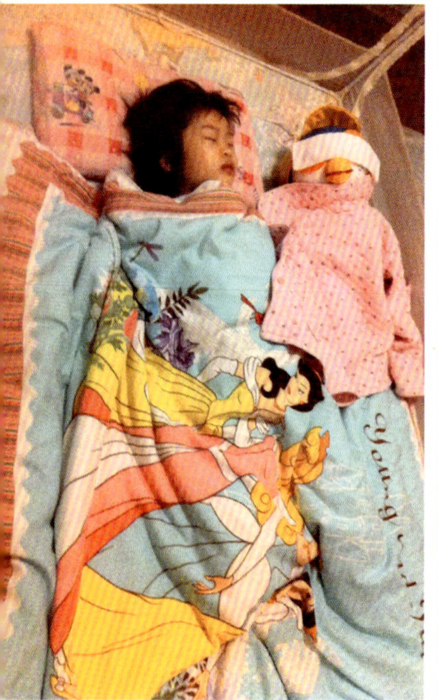

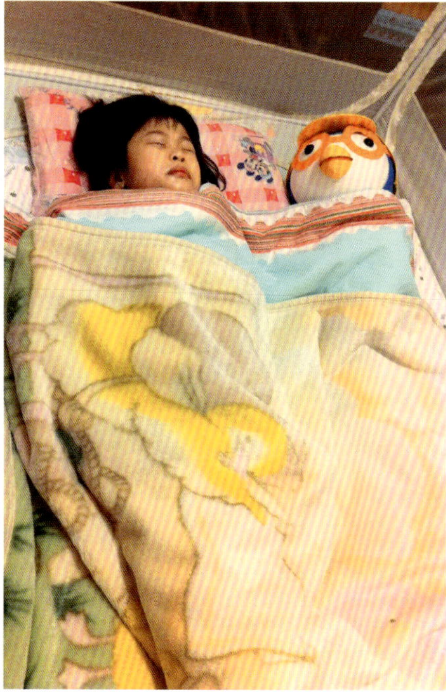

我和企鹅宝宝睡觉觉　I'm sleeping with baby penguin

外婆夸我种的芒果香又甜　Grandma praised my sweet mango

老师评价 Teacher's Comments

（二年级上学期）

莲子，看到你的名字就让老师想到那洁白无瑕的莲花，而你是那孕育着无限生命力的莲子。在你小小的世界里，你有善良、有天真、有分享、有幸福更有爱。对待数学，你一开始有点担心，怕自己回答错了，到后来你敢于尝试，老师能想象到你是鼓着多么大的勇气啊！当你勇敢地迈出第一步时，我看到了你脸上那种被肯定后美美的表情。

——数学老师 Math

You have been a great student Apple and I have seen a very big improvement jn your ability and confidence in English class. You have started to really open up in class and raise your hand to take part in the lessons.

——英语老师 English

可爱的你总是喜欢钻研，大树的叶子，掉落的花朵都能引起你注意力，你也曾告诉我许多关于大树和花朵的故事，那些故事真动听。在你的画面中让老师印象最深的是那幅水中奇景，你对水的画法把握得很到位，这样就使你的画面看起来像真的是从水底往上看一样震撼。

——选修课老师 Elective Course

妹妹这个学期明显的胆量大了，敢于发言了，会大声地说出自己对于作品的理解和想法，表演的时候，也会不甘人后的冲上讲台。考查完我问妹妹：为什么学习态度一栏少了一颗星？妹妹稚嫩的声音回答我说：因为我总是慢吞吞的来教室，总会迟到，总会看着窗户外边。呵呵，宝贝，对于自己有待改进的地方，你已经有了自觉，不着急，老师陪你一块儿慢慢长大！

——选修课老师Elective Course

这个学期你明显地爱上了回答问题，无论语文、数学还是英语课上，都能看到你坐直身体认真举手的样子，还记得那次讨论安全问题，你说得多好呀：“不要自作聪明，做该做的事。”让大家为你送上了热烈的掌声，你的小脸上也满是美丽的笑容。这样的莲子多可爱啊，就连这学期还会出现的“老先生”这个称呼，你的语气中所呈现的更多时候是亲密，而不再是如上学期那般的愤怒。看，恰恰是你心态的改变，让你笑得越来越美，本事越来越大。

——班主任老师Master Teacher

静静的你，不大爱说话。现在进步很大，吃饭时会自己主动夹菜了，而且吃饭的速度也稍有调整了。你学会了选择，吃饭时会自己吃多少装多少，不浪费，还帮家族做自己力所能及的事，拿碗筷、摆凳子、洗碗碟，你每次洗完碗后，便会到摆放筷子的地方把盘子里的筷子按类分好、摆整齐，然后才去教室。午休时即使睡不着，也不会影响别人。你沉浸在自己的世界里，快乐地生活着，我们更希望你把你的快乐和我们分享。

——生活老师Nursing Teacher

爸爸妈妈对你说 Parent's Comment

七岁的莲子：乖巧、懂事，自我管理的意识逐渐提升

莲子二年级第一学期结束了，爸爸妈妈在刚刚过去的学期里，开始感受到女儿成长带来的愉悦。七岁的莲子开始理解大人对她的要求，并且渐渐明白事理，能够自觉接受。

七岁的莲子乖巧、懂事，自我管理的意识逐渐提升。学期结束，爸爸妈妈觉得应该带莲子多出去走走，多看看外面的世界了。不长不短的寒假，妈妈与莲子商量安排的第一件事情就是去购书中心买书，对照学校布置的寒假作业，莲子挑选了英语、数学相关的书籍，还买了几本自己喜欢的童话书；接下来的第二件事情，便是莲子寒假学习的日子，妈妈与莲子相约：每天上午学习，下午自由安排活动，完成了假期作业，我们就去旅游。

过年前，莲子跟着爸妈开始了旅游的第一站——新加坡之旅；过年后，莲子跟着爸妈继续了旅游的第二站——海南三亚之旅。一路上，莲子从开始学习照相到将相机的各种功能使用到得心应手，出神入化。回到家里，对着照片写下了好几页纸的游记。

旅游行程的最后一天，我们将离开三亚返回广州，妈妈回想着开心快乐的每一天，感慨万千拉着莲子的小手说：“当爸爸妈妈渐渐老去的时候，会越来越怀念，今天带着宝贝女儿牵着你的小手到处旅游的快乐时光。”莲子听到顿时泪水涌出抱着妈妈哭了起来。

旅游的沿途，莲子不止一次对妈妈说，带着小孩真不容易！虽然是累，但爸爸妈妈永远珍惜与女儿相伴带给我们的幸福时光！

摘自《汇景新城实验小学学生素质发展评价表》

老师评价 Teacher's Comments

（二年级下学期）

你喜欢画画，在画的世界里，你很沉醉，说了许多的悄悄话，我知道莲子把画当成自己的好朋友。你知道上课应该干上课该干的事儿。有一次，莲子在积极举手回答问题后说：不想每天变笨一些，想变得更聪明，想变聪明就要努力学习！

——数学老师 Math

Apple, you have again been a very polite and happy student. You have attended every class with a lot of positive energy and joined in with class activities with a big smile on your face.1 have seen great progress in your spoken English and you are so often brave enough to raise your hand and give your answers in class.

——英语老师 English

Apple，在这个学期的英语话剧课中，体验到了不同的英语学习模式，相信也一定找到了其中的快乐。你经过自己的努力和锻炼，胆量越来越大了，也越来越有自信了。

——选修课老师 Elective Course

莲子，这个学期结束啦，你准备怎样评价自己呢？一定是笑眯眯地回答我一句“我不知道”吧？可是，每一个日子都是我们两个一起度过的，我记得清楚明白，相信你也一定不曾忘记！课堂上一次次高举的小手让老师们笑眯了眼睛，一定也让你开心不已吧？那不仅仅证明了你学会了知识，还记录了你成长的轨迹。每次看到你努力地思考，要找出别人没有的词语，都欣慰着，快乐着，这样的你是多么的可爱啊！

——班主任老师 Master Teacher

善解人意、乐于助人的你那一脸的真诚，让老师为之动容；你那满眼的关切，让同学们感到莫大的温暖。乐于助人更是你真正个性的体现，怎能忘记那些往事呢？你每天中午回到宿舍之后的第一件事情便是替大家将窗帘拉上，便于大家午休；起床时你又以飞一样的速度将窗帘打开，给大家带来光明。作为家族成员的一分子，你能尽自己的力量替家族做好自己该做的事情，如收拾餐桌、清洗餐具、参与家族的应聘工作。你一直在进步着，每天都在成长着。

——生活老师 Nursing Teacher

爸爸妈妈对你说 Parent's Comment

七岁的莲子：坚强、懂事，自我管理的能力很快提升

莲子二年级第二学期结束了，在这个学期，妈妈听到家长们说得最多的一句话便是“你们家的莲子进步很大”！

暑假，七岁的莲子同爸爸妈妈一起经历了一个人生跌宕的暑假！

七月，是个开心的日子，莲子自己选择了旅游线路，和爸妈一起，从广州—上海—苏州—上海—北京，经历了一个愉快而又丰富的旅程，在这个过程中，莲子既得到历练，又增长了知识。

八月二十日，即农历七月十四，这个中国传统的“鬼节”，对我们家来说真是个灾难的日子！当晚，经过全力抢救，莲子爸爸的生命总算从鬼门关被抢了回来！接下来的日子，妈妈每天总是提心吊胆奔波在医院、家里，每天看到妈妈拖着疲惫的身子从医院回到家，莲子总是想方设法让妈妈开心一点。但阿姨告诉妈妈，每当妈妈去医院的时候，莲子在家会偷偷地哭。

人生的灾难，让莲子一下子长大了好多，每天妈妈出门，她总会说：“妈妈，你去照顾爸爸，我在家会照顾好自己的，你放心！”每天妈妈从医院回来，她总会关切地询问：“爸爸现在怎么样了？”然后自己在家给爸爸画了很多祝福的画让妈妈带去医院给爸爸，知道爸爸不能吃东西，还画了爸爸最爱吃的水库大鱼头、老鸭汤等等。

七岁的莲子，已经成为爸爸妈妈面对灾难的精神支柱！

摘自《汇景新城实验小学学生素质发展评价表》

慎思·笃学　　厚德·博雅

奖状

程莲子

在2012-2013第一学期中，表现突出，

成绩优秀，荣获最具艺术创艺奖。

特发此状，以资鼓励！

匯景新城實驗小學
Favorview Palace Primary School

2013年1月17日

慎思·笃学　　厚德·博雅

奖状

程莲子

在2012-2013第一学期中，表现突出，

成绩优秀，荣获梨園新星奖。

特发此状，以资鼓励！

匯景新城實驗小學
Favorview Palace Primary School

2013年1月17日

慎思·笃学　　厚德·博雅

奖状

程莲子同学

在2012-2013学年第二学期中，表现突出，

成绩优秀，荣获小小话剧表演家奖。

特发此状，以资鼓励！

匯景新城實驗小學
Favorview Palace Primary School

2013年7月2日

慎思·笃学　　厚德·博雅

奖状

程莲子同学：

在2012-2013学年第二学期中，表现突出，

成绩优秀，荣获爱书人奖。

特发此状，以资鼓励！

匯景新城實驗小學
Favorview Palace Primary School

2013年7月2日

2014 · 展翅

Ready to Fly

美国斯坦福大学　Stanford University of the United States of America

你们常说：读万卷书，行万里路
所以，你们带着我，我带着笔，展开双翅
去北方看雪，去海角踏浪
跨大洋彼岸，游美国、狮城……
一幅幅绘画日记
怎么看都是一幅幅趣美图画

People say: Read ten thousand books and travel ten thousand Miles
So, you took me along and I took my paintbrushes
We flew to the north, watching snow
We went to the sea, taking a walk
We crossed the ocean, hailing U.S. and Singapore
Paintings were drawn like diaries
Depicting delightful happenings

作品点评

如果说程莲子之前的画不究技法的话，这幅《美丽花园》可说得上是一幅技法表现相当不错的画。整幅画面落色不杂，线条简练，虚实结合，主要以色块构图描物，那一片灰蓝色的爬墙植物和门窗与橙黄色的墙体衬比和谐，将作品的情调表现得别具一格。那辆小推车似点睛之笔，将花园主人热爱生活和劳动的形象不着痕迹地表现出来，可谓“此处无人胜有人”。

——张建平

Appreciation of Painting

If we say Cheng Lianzi did not use to draw by rules, this picture (*Beautiful Garden*) is indeed highly skilled. Generally, colors used are just the right amount and the lines are neat and simple. The fine combination of real and virtual scenes is also desirable. The painter mainly used color lumps to compose the picture. Particularly, the blue-grey wall plants, doors and windows are put in a delicate harmony with the orange walls, making the whole picture appear peculiar and exotic. What's most ingenious about this piece of work must be the little handcart. Without any noticeable trace, the painter delivered such a message: the owner of the garden is a lover of life and labor. Just as an old Chinese saying goes,"You say it best when you say nothing at all."

—Zhang Jianping

美丽花园 Beautiful Garden

奇幻园林 Fantasy Garden

作品点评

长满色彩缤纷奇花异草的绿地，矗立着几株苍劲挺拔的树木，树杆顶上，是如云如雾、灰绿迷蒙的团团叶冠，叶丛中，闪亮着红、蓝、黄、白、紫星星点点的花朵，给这片园林增添了一种奇幻神秘的色彩。这幅题为《奇幻园林》的画，将画境表现得颇为梦幻、神秘，很难想象是出于一个 9 岁女孩之手。画面所表现的境界别具一格，耐人寻味！

——张建平

Appreciation of Painting

Exotic flowers and rare herbs are blazing with color on the grassland. While the most eye-catching in this picture are some tall trees standing straight on the grassland. Looking up the top of the trunks, there are tree crowns like haze and clouds in dark green. See those shining spots hidden in the trees? Red, blue, yellow, white, purple... They are flowers glittering like stars, making the place more like in dream. This picture (*Fantasy Garden*) displays an illusory and mysterious style of painting, which triggers limitless imagination in the viewers. People can hardly believe a nine-year-old girl created such a piece of art.

—Zhang Jianping

花园别墅　Garden Villas

洛杉矶花园一角　A Corner of the Garden in Los Angeles

美国洛杉矶花园　A Garden in Los Angeles, American

花丛中有座桥　A Bridge Hidden in Flowers

春天到了 Spring is coming

数学本封面 Math Book Cover

夏天来了！ Summer is coming!

夏天来了，小朋友们去海边玩了
Summer's coming, let's go to the beach

太阳从东边升起 The Sun is rising in the east

美丽的公园 Beautiful Park

去海南　Next stop, Hainan

水果派对　Fruit Party

有莲　With Lotus

有节　With Bamboo

玫瑰公主　Princess Rose

白雪公主、阿拉丁、青蛙公主
Snow White, Aladdin, Frog Princess

童话故事中的少女 Little Girls in Fairy Tales

小美人鱼、花木兰、灰姑娘
Little Mermaid, Mulan and Cinderella

美丽少女 Beautiful Girls

巴啦啦小魔仙 The Fairy Balala

睡美人　Sleeping Beauty

灰姑娘　Cinderella

灰姑娘
Cinderella

睡美人
Sleeping Beauty

童话里的公主们　The Princesses in Fairy Tales

美人鱼有多美?

美人鱼有多美
Mermaid:"I don't know how beautiful I am."

大眼睛美人鱼
The Mermaid with Big Eyes

爱莉儿　Jilly

美丽的女孩从山里走过来
A beautiful girl always come from the mountains

可爱小女孩　Cute Little Girl

花木兰　Hua Mulan

女侠客　Female Knight

杨贵妃　Concubine Yang

宫女　Maid in Palace

古代少女　Ancient Girl

妈妈我爱你

妈妈我爱你　Mom, I love you

东南亚少女　Southeast Asian Girl

拿手链的小姑娘　The Little Girl Holding a Bracelet

杨梅
三年级自选课文
我爱故乡的杨梅
杨梅先是淡红,
随着就变深红,
因为它太红了
就黑了。它不是真的变黑了
你一口咬开,就可以看到新鲜的果肉了
汁水连牙齿都被染了。

摘杨梅　Picking Bayberry

小花仙　Flower Fairy

迪斯尼舞蹈秀

白色小公主

迪士尼舞蹈秀　Dancing at Disney

戴花的小姑娘　The Little Girl Wearing a Flower

动漫人物　Cartoon Characters

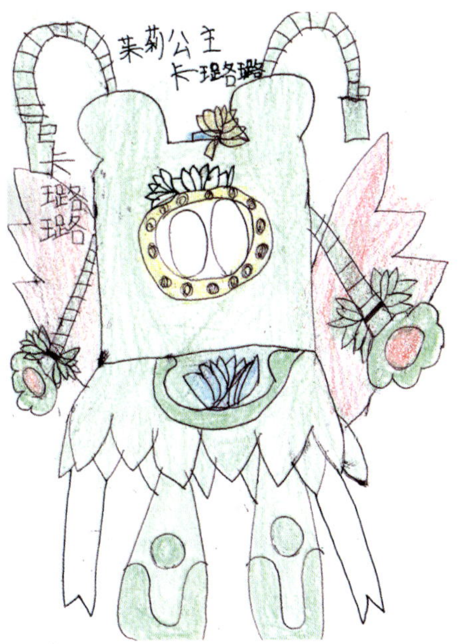

茉莉公主卡璐璐　Princess Jasmine Kalulu

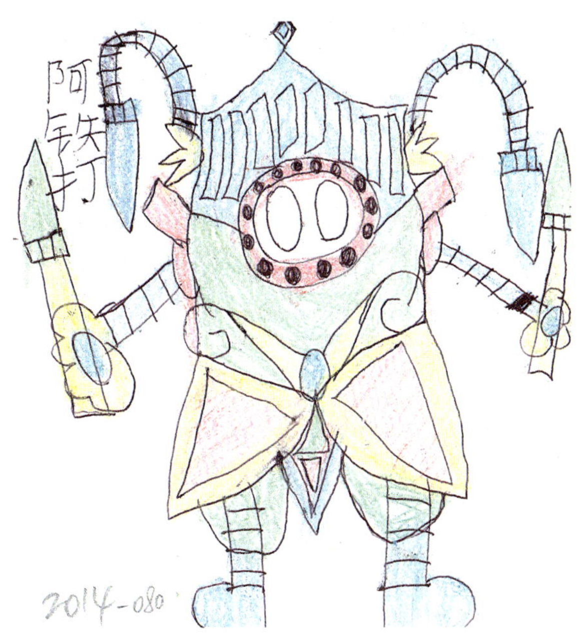

阿铁打　Atieda

池塘中的小金鱼　Little Goldfish in the Pond

送给妈妈的小鱼鱼　Little Fish for Mom

蓝色的鹦鹉　Blue Parrot

海底童话　Undersea Faïry Tales

怡红快绿　Lotus

窗边的小芽　The Budlet near the Window

向日葵　Sunflower

春天，夏天，秋天，冬天
Spring, Summer, Autumn and Winter

山茶花 Camellia

保护地球 Protecting the Earth

荷花 Lotuses

花朵上的蝴蝶 Butterflies Staying on the Flowers

花盆下的小蜗牛 Snail Under the Flowerpot

花儿开 Blooming Flower

圣诞快乐　Merry Christmas

万圣将军阿普　General Apu of Halloween

万圣节　Halloween

送给妈妈母亲节的礼物　Gift for Mother's Day

用废物（卷纸筒、纸巾和废纸）绘制的艺术品
Works of Art Drawn on Castoff (winding paper tube, facial tissue and waste paper)

上学去 Going to School

马航失联
Where is the Malaysia Airlines plane?

小豆芽 Small Bean Sprout

想象房间 Imaginative Room

服装设计 Fashion Design

秦汉发型 Hair Style of Qin and Han Dynasty

秦汉服饰 Clothes of Qin and Han Dynasty

秦汉服饰 Clothes of Qin and Han Dynasty

连环画：假日

Comics: Holiday

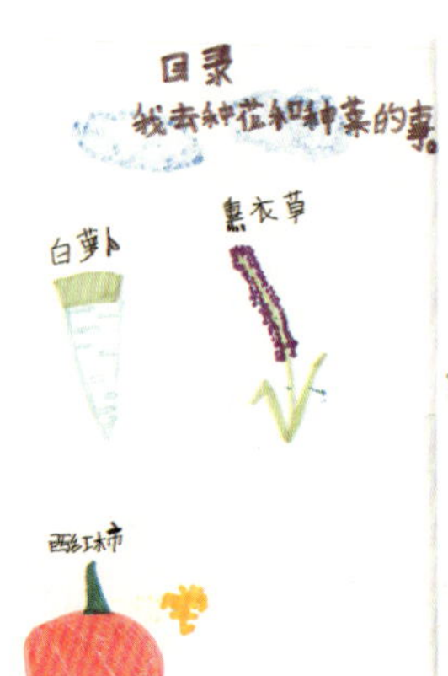

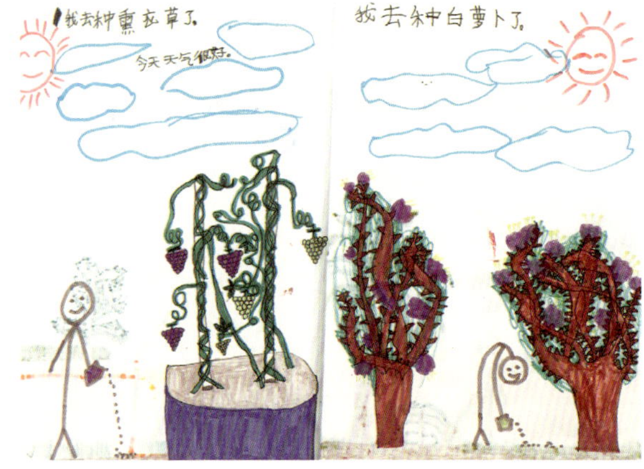

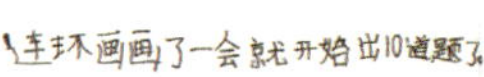

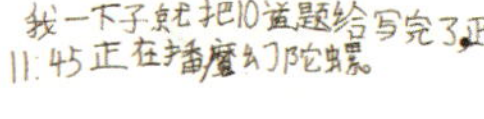

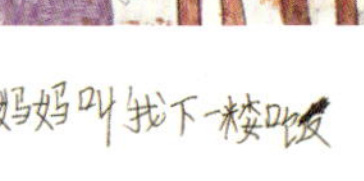

莲子：

看完你的假期作业，我太佩服你了。孩子，你对作业很认真，这种态度让人欣慰。其次，内容很丰富，简短的文字可感受到你假期生活的丰富，既跟植物亲密接触，又在家中做了很多事。这种表达真好，太棒了！再次，最让我佩服的是你的画太漂亮了，不仅构思优美，颜色搭配完美，你简直就是画画的天才啊！在上色与画图方面老师自愧不如！好好加油，老师看好你！未来的画家莲子！

最后，老师希望看到你更多的作品啊！本子发给你，可继续画哟！加油！

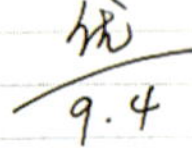

9.4

连环画：海岛游真好玩

Comics: Funny Island Tour

7月1日 晴 海南的

昨天，我在公园里，看到了一朵月季花。真漂亮！我把它拍了下来，高大又骄傲的椰子树，有着海滩的秘密

到了晚上，我在看冰雪奇原呢！

冰雪奇原播完了，我去游泳了

我游完泳后，就洗澡、刷牙、洗脸后就做达标卷里的语文题

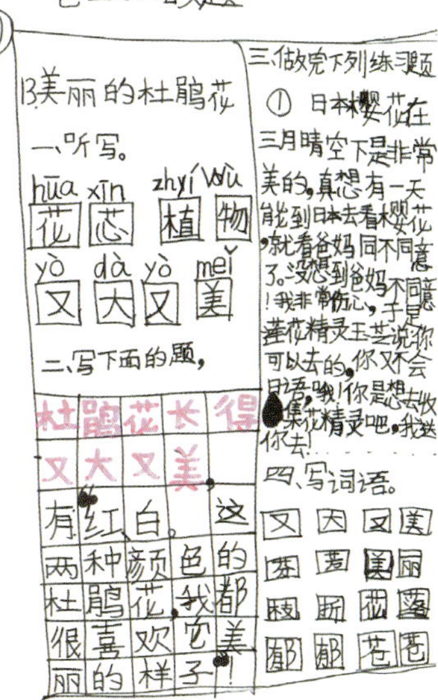

做完题后我上床了！

到了第二天早上，我起床、刷牙洗脸完后，我们下电梯吃早饭。

吃完早饭后，我们一家和吴敏阿姨一家一起去海底潜水，真好玩！

连环画：美国之旅

Comics: American Tour

上车了！
第一个目的地是金门公园 我们快到了
植物真不少！
我们到了
雷龙
我们进去了
雷龙

摄影作品

Photography Works

美国艺术之旅
Journey of Art in the United States of America

成长照片

Photos of Different Growth Phases

我喜欢凡·高的《鸢尾花》 I like Van Gogh's *Flower-De-Luce*

洛杉矶盖蒂博物馆 Gatti Museum, Los Angeles

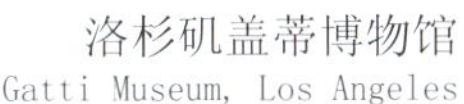

洛杉矶盖蒂博物馆
Gatti Museum, Los Angeles

旧金山艺术宫　Palace of Fine Arts, San Francisco

斯坦福大学艺术博物馆
Art Museum of Stanford University

斯坦福大学
Stanford University

跟妈妈去看艺术品拍卖
At the Art Auction with Mother

我爱艺术　I love art

我去三国赤壁古战场
Ancient Battlefield of the Three Kingdoms in Chibi

走在乡间小路上 Walking on a Country Road

2014/08/23

长隆游乐 Playing in Chimelong Water Park

我最爱亚龙湾 My Favorite Yalong Bay

公主裙好漂亮　The princess skirt is so beautiful

我是火车头　I am the head of the train

参观广东博物馆　Visiting Guangdong Museum

我是小厨师　I'm a little chef

扇舞——我的梦
Fan Dance - My Dream

老师评价 Teacher's Comments

（三年级上学期）

善良、有礼仪的你，现在越来越懂事了，能主动向老师行礼，向老师问好；每天都能准时地回到教室里，坐在自己的座位上，安安静静地做着自己的事情，不轻易去干扰别人，也不易被别人干扰。你喜欢在书上写题，整本数学书几乎都被你写完了，只是你不愿意把书交给我改，所以，我不知道你掌握知识的程度。孩子，我多想和你一起去探讨书上的习题啊，可你总不给我机会，希望你能给我机会，让我们一起去学习数学，研究数学，好吗？

——数学老师 Math

Apple2, you are a wonderful child. Your English is limited, yet you are able to use what English you have, along with hand gestures and facial expressions to express many of your thoughts and ideas, in a beautiful way. It would be great to have you be more actively involved in the classes. You often appear to not be listening, but then you surprise me with your sentences. which are often detailed, with some great vocabulary and excellent grammar, showing you"have absorbed what has been taught.

——英语老师 English

老师知道你是个非常热爱画画的孩子，从你的丙烯装饰画作品中我就能看出来，蓝蓝的背景和穿着漂亮裙子的公主站在船头上的组合，使人一下子就进入了美丽的童话故事里。或许是好奇心太强，你总希望去探寻外面的世界。老师总要在课前去找你，这样一来你就不能更快地完成更多的作品了，对于莲子这个小画家来说是多可惜的一件事情呀，因为老师真的希望能看到你更多出彩的绘画作品呢。

——选修课老师 Elective Course

刚开学的一段时间，莲子会站在队伍的边上做自己的事情，但随着时间的推移，莲子越来越多地加入到游戏中，甚至加入到设计游戏中，每一次你提出的点子，都引得老师给你一个大大的赞！因为我们莲子在用心思考与努力，而且你的点子太棒了，往往是出奇制胜的法宝！

——选修课老师 Elective Course

莲子，刚认识你的时候，你不是很容易让老师亲近的孩子。可是在跟你慢慢熟络之后，发现你其实很愿意与老师做朋友，很喜欢亲近他人，跟同学相处你也会有自己的办法表达出对他人的关心。你会把自己的课间水果留下来回家跟妈妈一起分享；如果来不及吃，你会把留下的橘子剥开跟同学分享，看着同学们吃完后笑得眼睛眯成一条线。开放周你给来到课室的同学的爸爸妈妈们装上一杯水，还甜美地说上：“叔叔阿姨请喝茶！”一些孩子的爸爸妈妈都称赞这个懂事的小姑娘。看到同学喜欢，你会把自己心爱的贺卡中的Hello Kitty分成好几块来送给同学，还不忘给老师也挑上一个。可是临近期末的时候，你受伤了，我们班上少了一个活蹦乱跳的身影，课间里少了一个叮嘱我们多喝水的声音，我们希望你在下个学期能顺顺利利地跟我们一起学习！

——班主任老师Master Teacher

莲子，能成为你的老师是件幸福的事情，还记得开学第一个午休吗？你静悄悄地靠在老师身边问：“老师，我很喜欢你，请问有什么工作可以帮忙的，我想长本事。”热心的请求让老师盛情难却，从此你便承担了为老师拉开窗帘唤醒起床的重要任务，有时还会耐心教一年级小学妹怎么整理床铺。在家族内，你能积极做好力所能及的工作，很享受打工的过程，每一个餐桌你都会仔细擦拭几遍，不留一颗饭粒。当老师情不自禁给予你肯定和称赞时，活泼的你立马回应一个调皮的笑脸，感谢有你这位热情开朗的开心果，给我们带来了许多的快乐。

——生活老师Nursing Teacher

写生 Painting from Life

爸爸妈妈对你说 Parent's Comment

八岁的莲子：开始经历成长中的人生磨难

2013 年 10 月 8 日，莲子八岁生日那天，是在没有爸爸陪伴中度过的。莲子提出要带上生日蛋糕去医院和爸爸一起度过自己八岁的生日，妈妈不同意时，莲子很坚决地表示，那我就等爸爸出院回来再过生日吧！

这个学期，莲子经历着成长中的人生磨难，生活发生了天翻地覆的巨变——之前每天送、接莲子上学、放学的爸爸整整一个学期几乎都是在医院里，莲子在家每每听到大人说到爸爸的病情，小小的心灵，常常也表现出担心、惊恐、害怕，好几次她告诉妈妈，我昨晚又发噩梦了。

整整一学期，妈妈几乎是无暇顾及莲子的学习和生活，甚至无法抽出时间陪伴莲子参加学校的亲子活动。当莲子大哭着问妈妈："为什么大家都有爸爸妈妈带着出去玩，而我却不可以？"妈妈听到心如刀割，觉得真的亏欠了孩子！

爸爸的生病，令到父母忽然间从人生的巅峰瞬间跌宕陷入低谷，因此而发生情绪的波动，心理的焦虑，心态的失衡等等，不可避免地给小小年纪的莲子带来一定的负影响。妈妈觉得，也许要考虑如何重新安排一个更加健康的环境以有利于莲子的成长。

12 月 10 日，莲子再度在学校跌伤，左腿骨裂导致无法行走，这学期余下的时间，莲子就在雪上加霜的日子里，常常是独自留在冷清的家里，不知如何度过这段漫长的时间。

2013 年的冬天似乎特别冷，而且冷得很漫长。2014 年的春天还是一如冬天般寒冷。总在期待着，阳光灿烂的日子早点到来，期盼阳光能带给孩子更多的温暖！

摘自《汇景新城实验小学学生素质发展评价表》

老师评价 Teacher's Comments

（三年级下学期）

越来越喜欢逐渐淡定、从容的莲子。课堂上，你慢慢找到上课的感觉，会独自地看书、思考、琢磨练习；碰到难题，你能突破自己去问老师，学会求助了，非要把不懂的弄懂，这种精神非常难得，继续保持哦。

——数学老师Math

Apple2, you rarely speak out in class, but you often come to speak to me after class. You have a wonderful way of making yourself understood, through a combination of your limited range of vocabulary, mixed with expression and gesture. Often, the conversation you make outside of class shows that you have, in fact, been listening during class when it appeared that you weren't. You are curious about the world, and you ask some interesting questions.

——英语老师English

你有与生俱来的色彩感，不管你画哪种类型的画，色彩方面都会让人很惊艳，在艺术方面你一直都很有主见，不会受他人的影响亦不会抄袭他人，所以长久以来，绘画方面形成了自有的风格，这可是很难得的。

——选修课老师Elective Course

来到咱们学校的第一天，就看到办公室桌上的画册，那是一个可爱的小女孩的作品，从那时起我就认识了你——莲子。去咱们班的第一天，你就拉着我的手，带我去校园看你最喜欢的鱼儿。你的亲近，让我感到很温暖，也让我开始了解莲子内心的纯净与美好。在你的书上、作文本上，常常可以看到很多漂亮可爱的小插图，这些图画，充满着童真与想象力，让老师看到莲子的世界是充满着那么多的真、善、美。

——班主任老师Master Teacher

曾经是活泼开朗、人见人爱的开心果，如今是理性、从容、善解人意、有责任感的小学姐。聪明的你懂得什么时间该做什么事情，一次午餐，一位族员在餐桌前着急地等候着老师过来交接餐具，在她身边认真擦桌子的你扭过头来微笑地对她说：“要不你先回课室阅读，待会儿让我来帮你交接吧。”学妹高兴得连声道谢，俏皮可爱的你淡定而优雅摇着头回应道：“我们都是一个家族的，不用客气。”只见你用抹布把餐桌擦得干干净净，然后把刚洗过的餐具分类摆到餐桌上清点，做事情用心认真的莲子有种不一样的美。亲爱的小莲子，用你的真诚善良、乐观坚强、豁达大度作为明灯，相信前方的路一定是光明而灿烂的！

——生活老师Nursing Teacher

爸爸妈妈对你说 Parent's Comment

八岁的莲子：开始在人生磨难中成长

依然只有八岁的女儿，在过去的一年，与家人一起经历了人生的磨难后已经懂得理解，体谅，分担。漫长的暑假，莲子虽然非常渴望出去旅游，或期待妈妈多点在身边陪伴自己，但即使偶尔能跟随妈妈出去，看着妈妈忙碌的身影，她也只是安安静静地在一旁做自己的事情。

在家里，莲子已经开始与妈妈分担照顾爸爸的责任，每当爸爸咳嗽，就跑去帮爸爸拍背，看到爸爸出汗，就会给爸爸递上毛巾，并且懂得提醒爸爸能吃什么、不能吃什么等等。

快开学了，莲子终于盼到妈妈可以带自己去家门口的长隆水上乐园玩上一天，开心得不得了！当妈妈颇为内疚地向女儿说“对不起！”时，还是八岁的女儿却安慰妈妈说：“妈妈，我已经很满足了！”

有一天，莲子忽然问：“妈妈，为什么我每次考试成绩都是那么差呢？”妈妈心感欣慰地说：“女儿，当你意识到了自己的不足，能够加以努力，相信一定会进步的！”

宝贝，加油！

摘自《汇景新城实验小学学生素质发展评价表》

慎思·笃学

奖状

程莲子

在2013-2014学年上学期中，表现突出，

成绩优秀，荣获爱岗敬业小能手奖。

特发此状，以资鼓励！

匯景新城實驗小學

Favorview Palace Primary School

2014年1月8日

厚德·博雅

慎思·笃学

奖状

程莲子

在2013-2014学年上学期中，表现突出，

成绩优秀，荣获快乐分享美德女孩奖。

特发此状，以资鼓励！

匯景新城實驗小學

Favorview Palace Primary School

2014年1月8日

厚德·博雅

慎思·笃学

奖状

程莲子

在2013-2014学年上学期中，表现突出，

成绩优秀，荣获礼仪小天使奖。

特发此状，以资鼓励！

匯景新城實驗小學

Favorview Palace Primary School

2014年1月8日

厚德·博雅

慎思·笃学

奖状

程莲子

在2013-2014年第二学期中，表现突出，

成绩优秀，荣获感情真挚朗诵家奖。

特发此状，以资鼓励！

匯景新城實驗小學

Favorview Palace Primary School

2014年7月1日

厚德·博雅

慎思·笃学

奖状

程莲子

在2013-2014年第二学期中，表现突出，

成绩优秀，荣获爱心大使奖。

特发此状，以资鼓励！

匯景新城實驗小學

Favorview Palace Primary School

2014年7月1日

厚德·博雅

慎思·笃学

奖状

程莲子

在2013-2014年第二学期中，表现突出，

成绩优秀，荣获色彩大师奖。

特发此状，以资鼓励！

匯景新城實驗小學

Favorview Palace Primary School

2014年7月1日

厚德·博雅

2015 · 寻梦

Pursuing My Dreams

艺术殿堂　The Palace of Art

十岁，是爱美的年龄
十岁，是多梦的时光
带着美丽的艺术梦想
奔向美好的未来……

At ten, I'm seeking beauty
At ten, I'm pursuing dreams
With arts
With visions
I'm heading for a bright future

作品点评

变形的四肢，抽象的几何图，繁杂的色块，遍布的眼睛……小画家想要表达什么呢？我们不得而知，但也无妨可以这样理解：世界形形色色，社会纷纷攘攘，生活丰富多彩，但眼睛却无处不在。是世俗的漠视？是好奇的探究？还是执著的前瞻……这是一幅色彩艳丽、构图新颖的图画，透过看似平和的画面，可联想某些生活中的深意。当代观念艺术就是这样，作品出来了，如何理解可以见仁见智。只是一个不到十岁的小女孩，能够如此成熟地表现观念艺术，不得不令人刮目相看。

——张建平

Appreciation of Painting

This picture is shocking with strong, bright colors and a novel composition. Beneath the seemingly obscure surface hides certain deep thinking about life. Distorted arms and legs, abstract patterns, various colors and scattered eyes...what does the little painter mean to express? The answer is nowhere to be found. But it does no harm to try to encode the picture: the world is so inclusive to be of every description; the society is crowded with numerous people and everlasting secular affairs. Life, is always charming with all wonderful possibilities it has to offer. However, there are eyes watching, here and there. Is this ignoring of secular human world? A desire to look into the unknown? Or just unceasing foresight into the future? ...Such is contemporary conceptual art. When a piece of work comes out, it is ready to embrace varying comments. However, a girl under ten is capable of expressing conceptual art in such a sophisticated manner. That is really amazing!

—Zhang Jianping

抽象拼体　Abstract Pieces

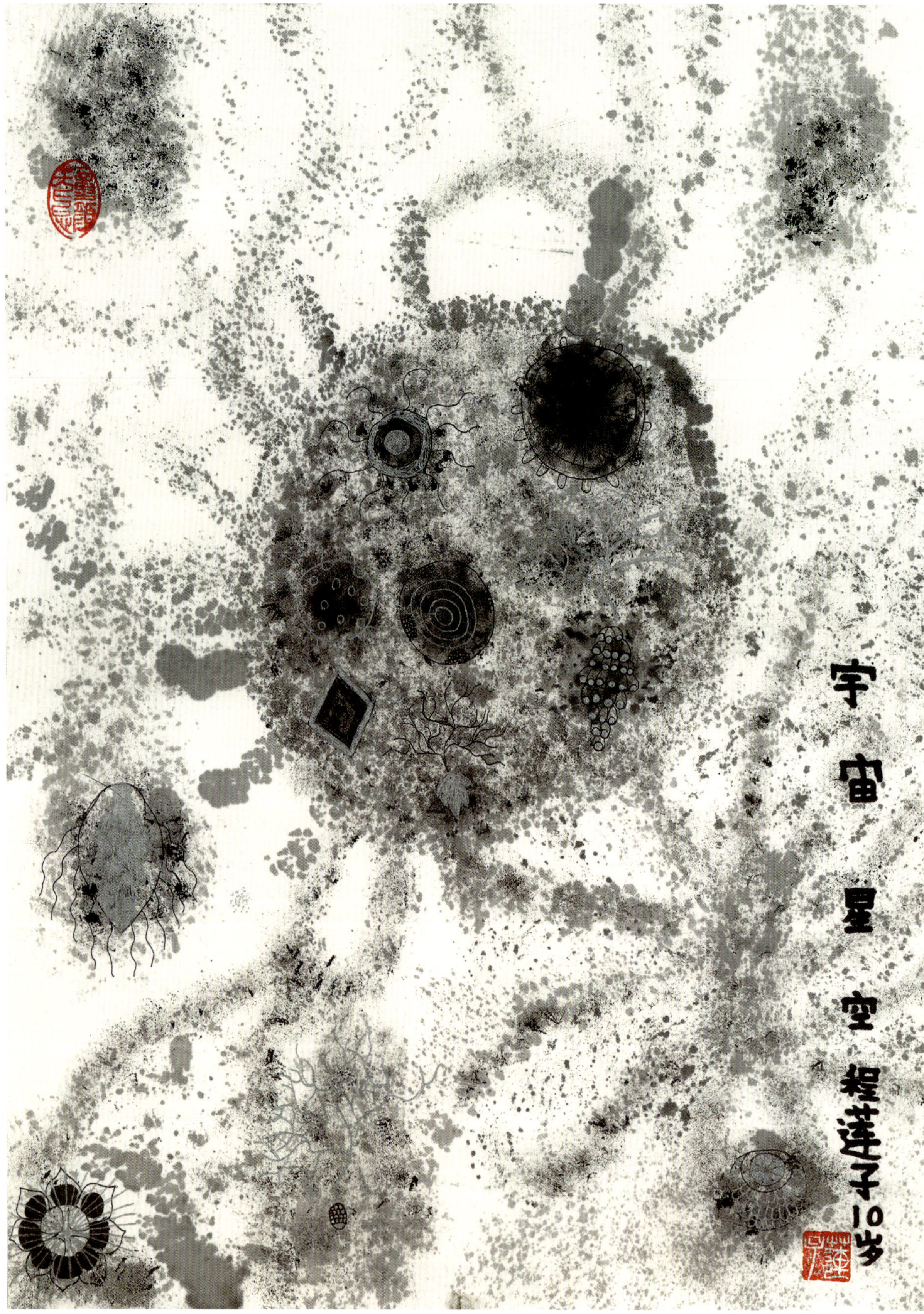

宇宙星空 Universe and Stars

作品点评

一个十岁小女孩以宇宙星空作为绘画主题，本身就非常罕见，不知是什么触动了她的灵感。此画的精趣之处不仅在于有黑窟窿的球体与一片网状物质的联系，这是一个小孩所理解的宇宙和星空，而在于她将这片宇宙星空描画得空灵而虚幻，为了表现这种空灵虚幻，她放弃了小女孩通常喜欢的多彩多色，选择了单一的黑白色，并且刻意将画面处理得混沌模糊，因此而将空灵虚幻的意境表现得更为极致。可见小画家已经不满足于单纯构图，而是着意表现某种意境和某些观念了，这是绘画走向成熟的可喜表现。

——张建平

Appreciation of Painting

It is not common for a ten-year-old girl to draw on the topic of universe and stars. So what has triggered the painter's interest? The subtlety of this picture does not only lie in the connection between the sphere with black holes and the net-like material around it. This is a little child's understanding about the universe and the stars. The charm lies in the way the little painter depicts the starry sky——vague and illusory. For this, she gave up fancy colors most little girl might use. Instead, she only picked white and black as the main keynote, and purposefully make the picture vague and hazy so as to take the feeling of dream and eternity to an extreme. Apparently, our little painter is not contended with simple composition of a picture, but tries to endow her picture with some artistic conceptions and in-depth meanings. This is a pleasant sign of becoming mature in painting.

—Zhang Jianping

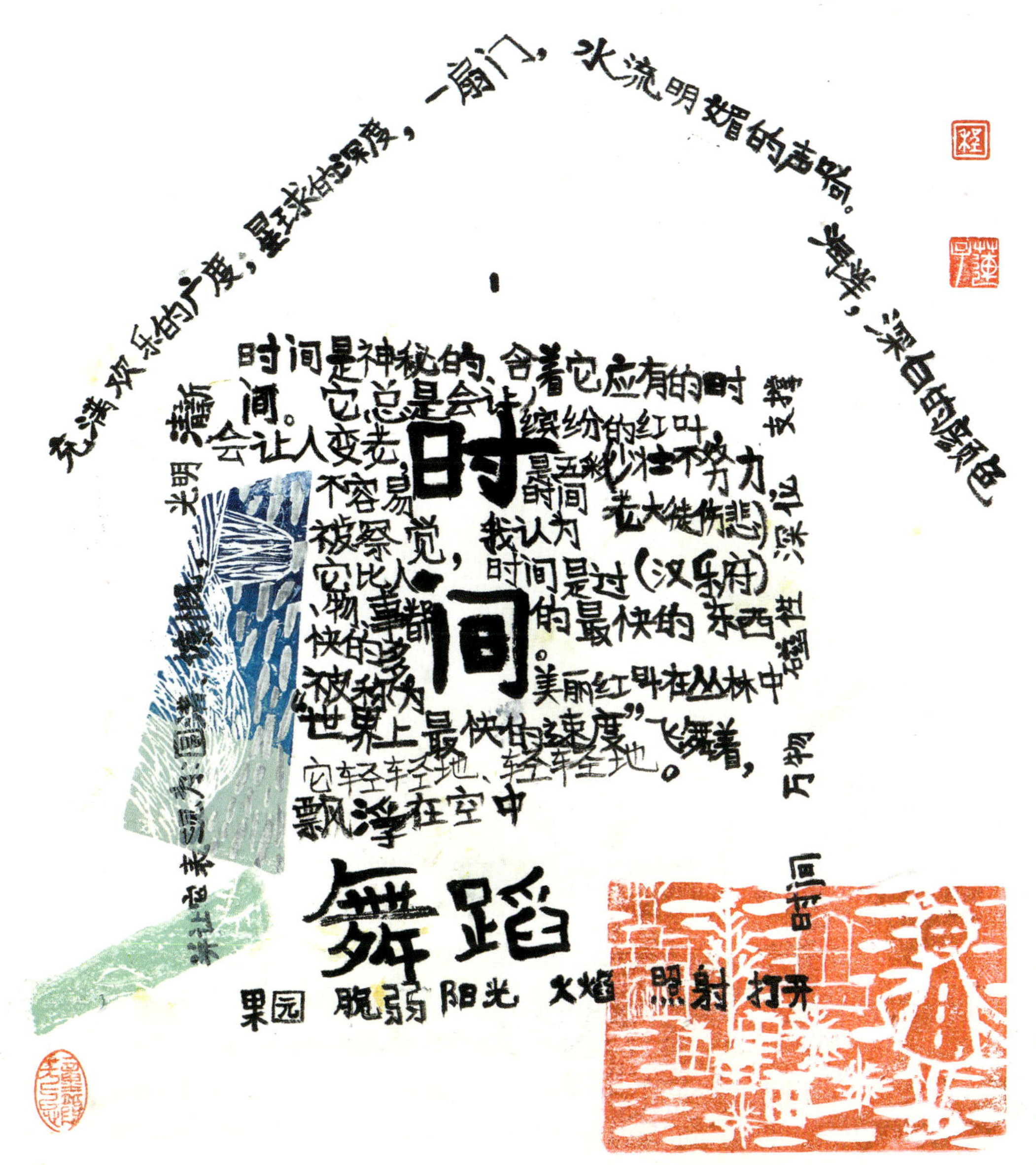

和时间赛跑　Racing with Time

窗边种满了花 Flowers near the Window

有特点的建筑　Special Architecture

秘密花园　Secret Garden

奇妙的小花园 Wonderful Garden

树荫下的大卡车 The Lorry Under the Tree

春天来了 Spring is coming

清明节，家乡游
Tomb-Sweeping Day in My Hometown

祖屋 Ancestral House

2015 年的春天 Spring of 2015

清风明月本无价，近水遥山皆有情
Invaluable Wind and Moon, Lovely Water and Mountain

月光仙子 Moonlight Fairy

海中的小船 Boat on the Sea

中秋的圆月 Full Moon on Mid-Autumn Day

中秋节的一天 Mid-Autumn Day

绿化森林 Green Forest

音乐午餐　Lunch with Music

妈妈回家了　Mom's back home

鸟语花香　Singing Birds and Fragrant Flowers

一个女孩的彩色世界　A Girl's World of Colors

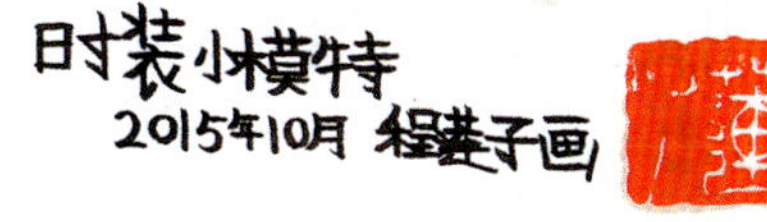

时装小模特　Fashion Models

一家人去海南 Family Tour in Hainan

我们永远在这个花园里 We will never leave the garden

好姊妹　Good Friends

凌美雪海报　Poster of Lin Meixue

小人书　Picture-Story Book

一家三口最幸福　A Most Happy Family!

我去学游泳　Learning to Swim

得金奖啦　I won the gold award!

表情　Expressions

三个花仙子　Three Flower Fairies

中国、日本、印度服装
Chinese, Japanese and Indian Costumes

美丽花仙子　Beautiful Flower Fairy

哪吒闹海　Naughty Nezha stirs the sea

秦朝公主 The Qin Dynasty Princess

明朝女皇
The Queen of the Ming Dynasty

廖明琳像 Portrait of Liao Minglin

古代少女 Ancient Girl

三个少女 Three Girls

《红楼梦》人物
Characters in *Dream of Red Mansions*

荷花少女 Lotus and Girl

休闲装 Casual Style

华美装 Gorgeous Style

可爱装 Cute Style

漂亮的女孩 Beautiful Girl

美丽花仙子
Beautiful Flower Fairy

精灵 Fairy

玩蛇的女孩
The Girl Playing with Snake

杨贵妃　Yang Concubine

貂蝉　Diao Chan

王昭君　Wang Zhaojun

西施　Xishi

精密计划：救人
Great Plan: Rescuing!

海洋之旅 Marine Journey

梨小平、梨小红、桃花江平、华小黑、三元钱一队。

喵星人金吉拉　Cat Chinchilla

时尚动物　Fashionable Animals

大白鲨 White Shark

奶牛 Cow

快乐的小鱼 Happy Fish

玩毛线的喵星人 Cat Playing with Woolen Yarn

梅　Plum Blossom

花园里的旋律 Melody in the Garden

鲜花与可乐　Flowers and Coke

梦幻玫瑰　Dream Rose

玫瑰花项链　Rose Necklace

茉莉花项链　Jasmine Necklace

美丽鲜花　Beautiful Flowers

小花苍苍　Small Flower

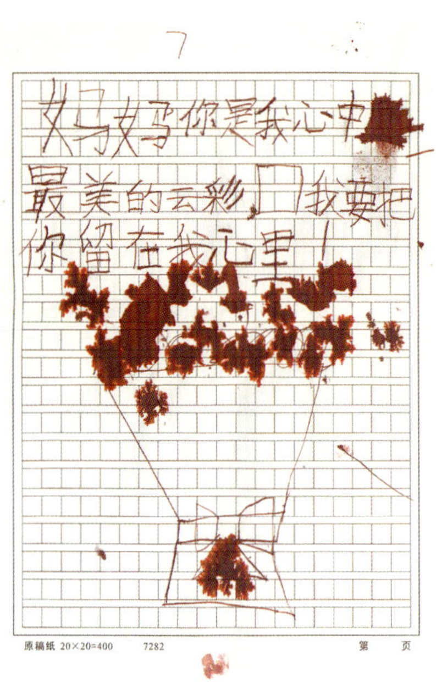

妈妈你是我心中最美的云彩
Mom is the most beautiful cloud in my heart

木槿花　Shrub Althea Flower

康乃馨　Carnation

阳光下的小花　Flowers in the Sunshine

荷花练习专用本封面　Book Cover of Lotus Painting

铅笔宝宝　Pencil Baby

艺术字母　Artistic Letters

神奇的齿轮　Magical Toothed Gear

野餐的食物　Food for Picnic

坏海盗，看我不教训你！　Bad Pirate, I will beat you!

荷花的故事 The Story of Lotus

爱漂亮的蛇
Snake:"Why can't I look pretty?"

戴皇冠的美人鱼
The Mermaid Wearing a Crown

哪吒闹海 Naughty Nezha stirs the sea

喵星人 Cat

猫怎么会变成枪?
How could a cat become a gun ?

小姑娘 Little Girl

月光少女 Moonlight Girl

吉祥仙子 Lucky Fairy

瓜菜 Vegetables

花园小屋 Garden Cottage

花仙子 Flower Fairy

海底世界　The World under the Sea

蘑菇有毒　Poisonous Mushrooms

水果　Fruits

和爸爸妈妈划船　Boating with Mom and Dad

想象房子　Imaginative House

池诗写　Pond, Poem and Paint

参观三国亭　Visiting the Three Kmgdoms Pavilion

作息时间表　My Schedule

春夏秋冬　Spring, Summer, Autumn and Winter

《秘密花园》书签设计
Design of Bookmark: the Secret Garden

荷花、莲藕、胖头鱼 Lotus, Lotus Root, Variegated Carp

小鸭　Duck

孔雀　Peacock

火鸡　Turkey

斑马　Zebra

小胖猪　Fat Pig

乌龟　Turtle

速写之旅
Journey of Sketch from Nature

大树下 Under the Big Tree

妈妈和宝宝 Mom and Baby

远处看着摩星岭
Seeing the Moxing Mountain from far

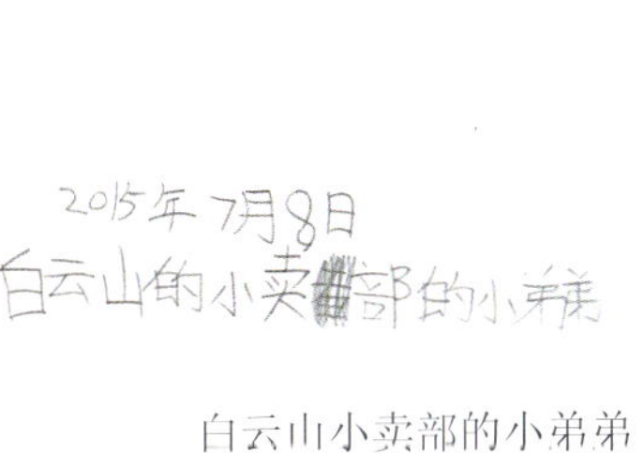

白云山小卖部的小弟弟
Little Boy at Baiyun Mountain Canteen

游双溪 A Visit to Shuangxi

感冒的女孩 Girl with a Cold

广州塔 Guangzhou Tower

百万葵园写生
Painting from Life in the Sunflower Garden

向日葵 Sunflower

凤洋仙 Balsamine

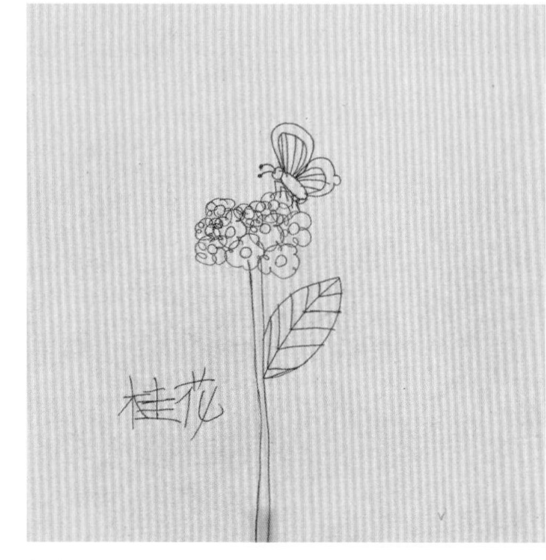

桂花 Fragrans

桃花 Peachblossom

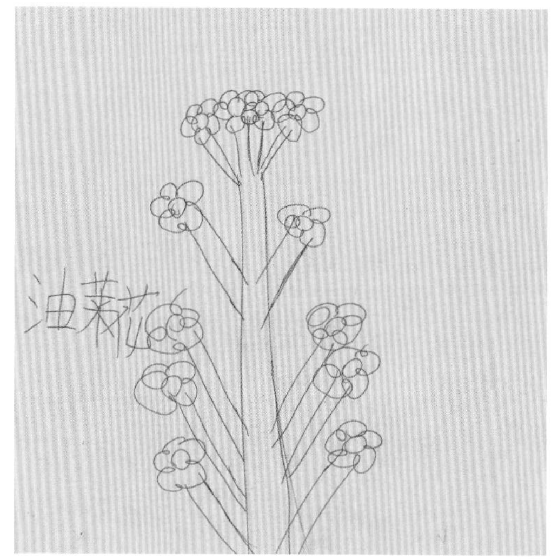

油菜花 Cole Flowers

玫瑰花 Rose

竹子 Bamboo

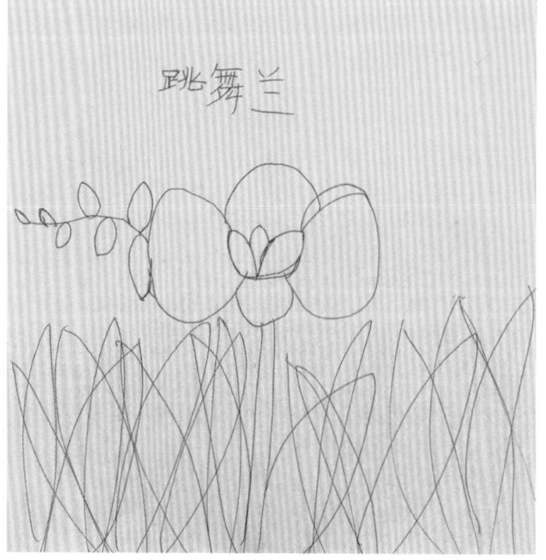

跳舞兰 Oncidium

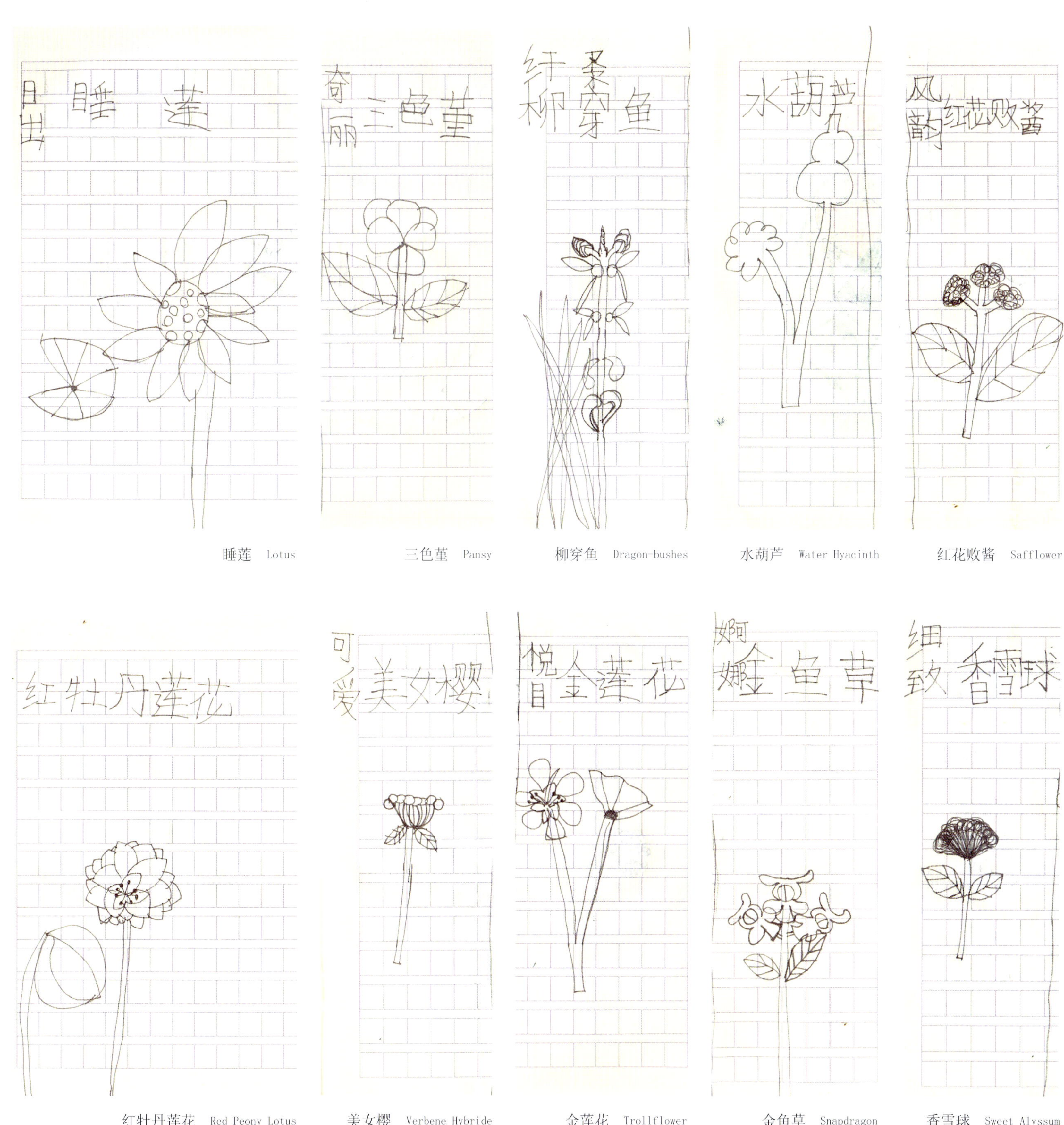

睡莲 Lotus

三色堇 Pansy

柳穿鱼 Dragon-bushes

水葫芦 Water Hyacinth

红花败酱 Safflower

红牡丹莲花 Red Peony Lotus

美女樱 Verbene Hybride

金莲花 Trollflower

金鱼草 Snapdragon

香雪球 Sweet Alyssum

钢琴的烦恼 Annoyance of the Piano

程莲子在创作《钢琴的烦恼》
Lianzi is making the "Annoyance of the Piano"

作品点评

这是一个装置艺术，很有小女孩的特点：造型小巧玲珑，色彩层次丰富，结构整齐有序。但如果不细究上面的文字和音乐符号，很不容易理解小画家创作的本意。一排像是钢琴键盘的前面，放着一张老师的座位，一张学琴小孩的座位，后面立着的小纸片上画着五线谱，音符上画着一些红色圈圈，那通常是老师批改作业时表示错误的符号，似乎表现教琴老师常在批评她“弹错了……”纸片后面是丛生的荆棘，旁边是一张床，前面是色彩鲜艳的幸运星，指向前方……如何选择是好？？？好了，无需多说了，学琴小童的烦恼无奈和面对艰难选择的纠结跃然而出，趣味盎然。其实这种学习的烦恼与选择的困顿在小孩子成长的各个时期又何尝不是如此呢？这个装置表现的问题在当今中国很具有普遍意义，其表现的方式既令人啧啧称奇，又让人感到童趣无限，很难不让人报以会心一笑，并对其丰富的想象力和表现力给予一赞！

——张建平

Appreciation of Painting

This is a set of handicraft designed with great artistic aesthetics, which is integrated with a little girl's characteristics: The whole model is mini and exquisite with rich gradation of colors. The neat layout of the small items makes this piece of art pleasing to the eye. But if the characters and musical notes on the paper are not carefully read, we may fail to understand the little painter's real intention behind.

Before a row of keyboard-like gadget are two seats for the piano teacher and the pupil (supposedly). Right behind that stands a tiny piece of paper with stave on it, and there are marked red circles on the stave. These red circles are generally used by teachers to point out the mistakes made in a student's homework. Seeing these signs, we can't help but imagine the scene that the piano teacher keeps criticizing her young pupil "It's wrong here...wrong..." . A clump of thorn is placed behind the piece of paper. And next to the thorn we can see a lovely bed in a spoon. On the northwest corner, two lucky stars are "looking" far into the distance from the top of a pole. "Where should I go?" The little pupil's annoyance and frustration as well as the bitter struggle before a hard choice are all vividly portrayed. This is extraordinarily interesting, and, affecting. The arduous journey of learning together with tough choices never fail to frustrate young children. However, such frustration will probably keep them company at every stop along the way they grow up. The appeal of children reflected through this handicraft has universal significance in the current Chinese society. On the one hand, we are fascinated by the ingenious creativity of the little artist; on the other hand, we cannot resist the temptation to laugh good-humoredly for the innocence and interest enjoyed from this artistic creation. Who could ever grudge giving her applause for such wonderful imagination and expressiveness?

—Zhang Jianping

橡皮泥手工：圣诞树
Plasticine Christmas Tree

花瓣剪贴画：时装模特　Petals Clipart : Fashion Models

人物剪纸　Paper Cutting of Characters

玫瑰花园送给爸妈　Rose Garden for Mom and Dad

送给外婆的立体画：恐龙世界
Stereograph for Grandma: Dinosaur Paradise

摄影作品

Photography Works

澳洲艺术之旅　Tour of Art in Australia

RENTALS

WELCOME
REFUGEES

WELCOME

三亚风光　Picturesque Scenery in Sanya

香港：海上日出　Hongkong; Sunrise on the Sea

成长照片

Photos of Different Growth Phases

参加广东美术馆培训中心 15 周年展览

Attending the 15 Anniversary of the Guangdong Art Museum Training Center

好多人，好多画
Mountains of People,
Mountains of Pictures

认识毕加索　I Know Picasso

我也是“思想者”　I am also a “thinker”

我好喜欢这幅画　I like it!

这是艺术殿堂　The Palace of Art

悉尼歌剧院　Sydney Opera House

库克船长小屋　Captain Cook's Cottage

悉尼大桥　Sydney Harbour Bridge

去香港看巴塞尔艺术展
Art Basel in Hongkong

参观中国国家博物馆副馆长陈履生伯伯展览
At the Art Exhibition of Uncle Chen Lvsheng,
Vice Curator of National Museum of China

我最爱画画　I love painting best

其实我不太喜欢弹钢琴，但我的老师很好　I don't like piano, but I have a good teacher

我教爸爸跳舞　Dad, follow me to dance!

和同学一起表演歌舞　Performing Singing and Dancing with My Classmates

裁判员

校运会，爸爸在主席台看我当旗手
I was a flag escort at school sports day
Dad's watching from the auditorium

我的教室 My Classroom

课间操 Exercise Between Classes

课间休息 Rest Between Classes

公开课 Open Class

青青果家族，我是族长
I am patriarch of the Grenco Family

学做菜　Learning to Cook

劳动最光荣　Labor is the glorious work

过新年，收利是 Lucky Money, Lucky New Year

喜欢下雪的北京 I love Beijing in snow

好可爱的洋娃娃 What a lovely toy!

老家的菠萝树 Pineapple Tree in My Hometown

蓝天下的我 Blue Sky over My Head

妈妈说我是小书迷 Mom calls me little bookworm

妈妈送我十岁的生日礼物
Ten-Year-Old Birthday Gifts from Mom

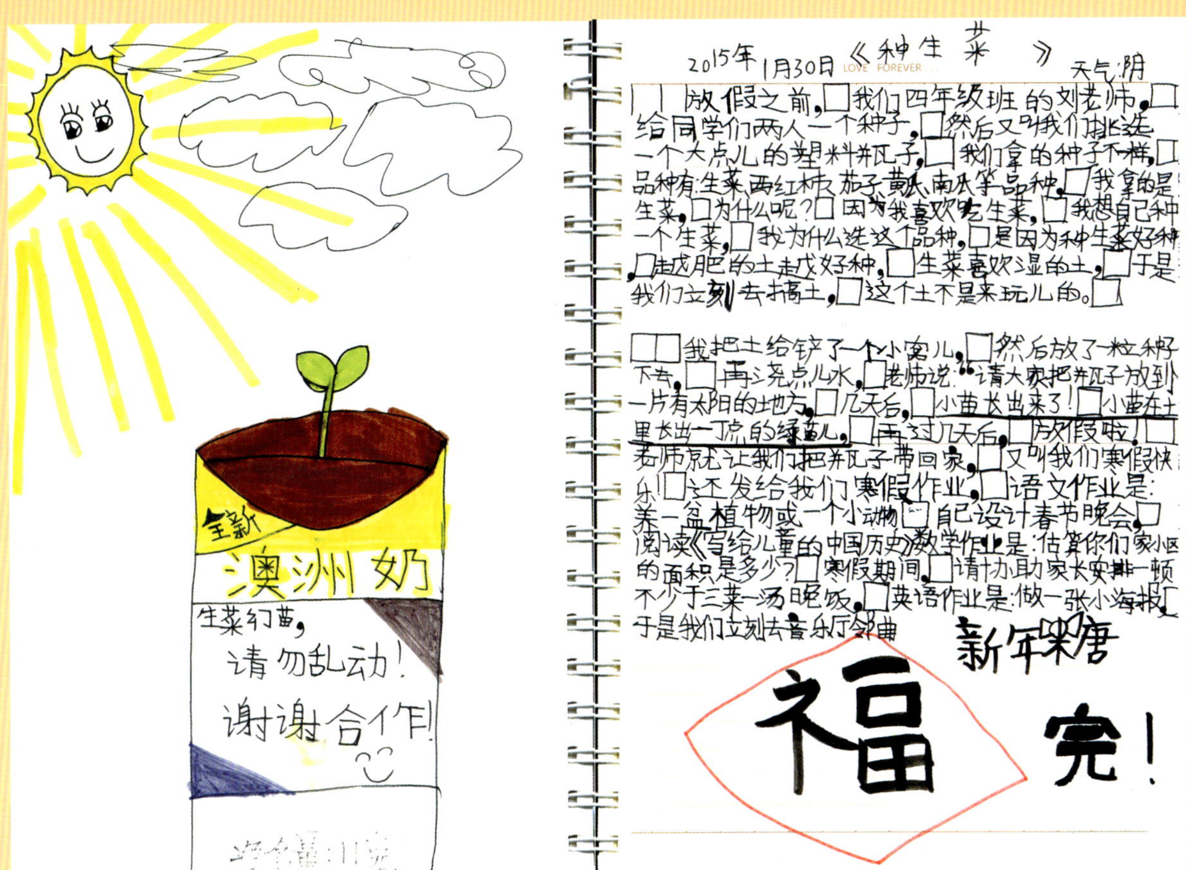

2015年1月30日《种生菜》天气:阴

放假之前,我们四年级班的刘老师,给同学们两人一个种子,然后又叫我们挑选一个大点儿的塑料瓶子,我们拿的种子不一样,品种有:生菜、西红柿、茄子、黄瓜、南瓜等品种,我拿的是生菜,为什么呢?因为我喜欢吃生菜,我想自己种一个生菜,我为什么选这个品种,是因为种生菜好种,越肥的土越好种,生菜喜欢湿的土,于是我们立刻去搞土,这个土不是来玩儿的。

我把土给铲了一个小窝儿,然后放了一粒种子下去,再浇点儿水,老师说:"请大家把瓶子放到一片有太阳的地方。"几天后,小苗长出来了!小苗在土里长出一丁点的绿苗儿,再过几天后,放假啦!老师就让我们把瓶子带回家,又叫我们寒假快乐!还发给我们寒假作业,语文作业是:养一盆植物或一个小动物,自己设计春节晚会,阅读《写给儿童的中国历史》数学作业是:估算你们家小区的面积是多少?寒假期间,请协助家长安排一顿不少于三菜一汤晚饭,英语作业是:做一张小海报,于是我们立刻去音乐厅听曲

福

完!

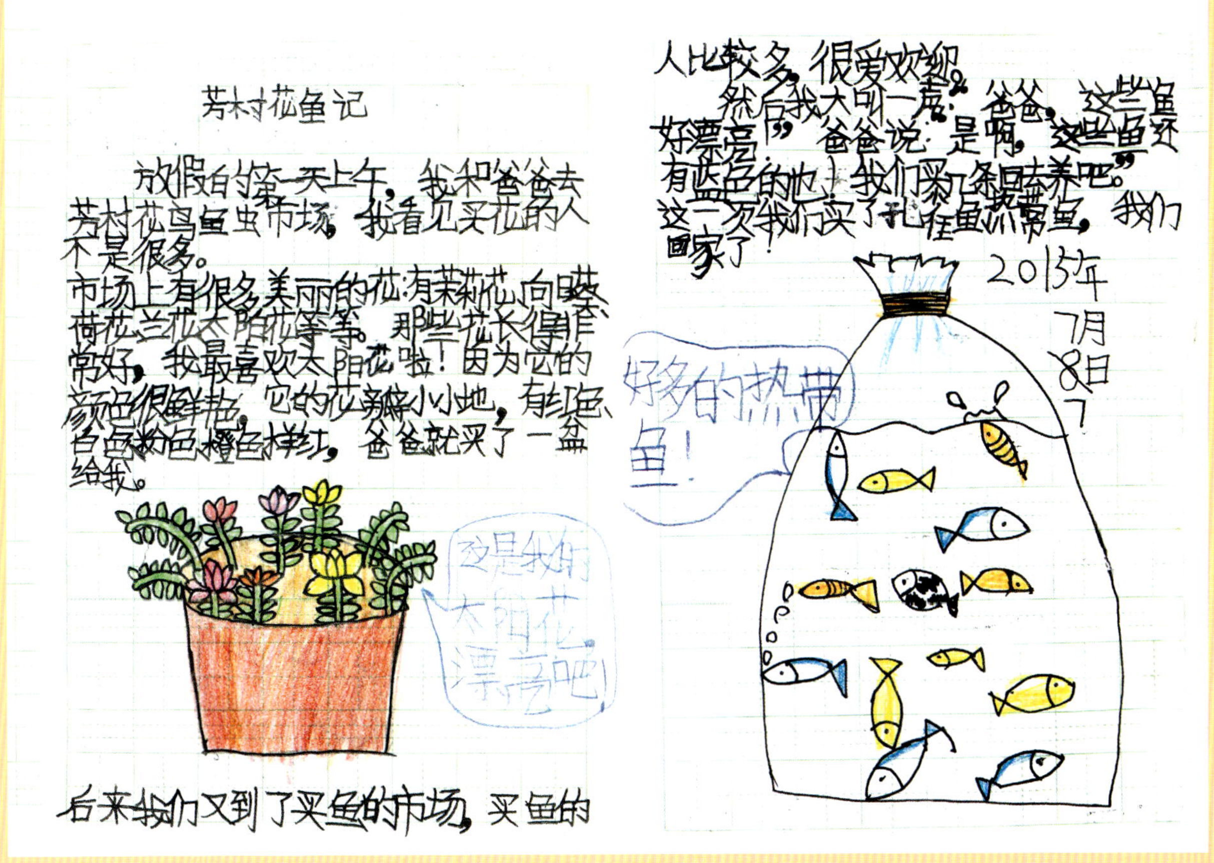

芳村花鱼记

放假的第一天上午,我和爸爸去芳村花鸟鱼虫市场,我看见买花的人不是很多。

市场上有很多美丽的花:有茉莉花、向日葵、荷花、兰花、太阳花等等。那些花长得非常好,我最喜欢太阳花啦!因为它的颜色很鲜艳,它的花瓣小小地,有红色、白色、粉色、橙色样样,爸爸就买了一盆给我。

后来我们又到了买鱼的市场,买鱼的人比较多,很受欢迎。

然后我大叫一声:"爸爸,这些鱼好漂亮!"爸爸说:"是啊,这些鱼还有蓝色的也!我们买几条回去养吧。"这一次我们买了几条热带鱼,我们回家了!

2015年7月8日

白云山上的"模特"

放假的第二天，今天天气是阴天，太阳一直没有露面。白云山上一直都是凉爽的，爬山的人会感觉很舒服。

我和爸爸下了车，走着走着，我们就走到了山顶。我就把爸爸骗到舅爷那去，我就找了个阴凉又隐蔽的地方给一个阿姨和一个小弟弟画了一幅速写画。

然后我就拿了这幅画给舅爷看，舅爷可是全国著名大画家之一，舅爷说"画得非常好"。

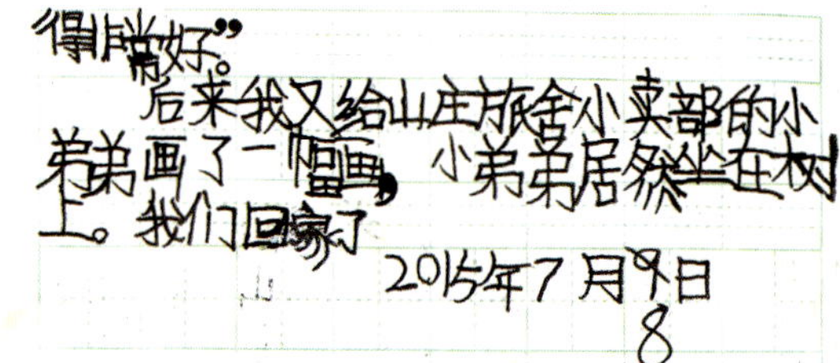

后来我又给山庄旅舍小卖部的小弟弟画了一幅画，小弟弟居然坐在树上。我们回家了。

2015年7月9日

8

满楼书香

因为暑假作业要求买一本字帖，所以我和爸爸去了广州购书中心。

购书中心大门就像一张大嘴，把人吸进去了。进入后，会感觉到很凉爽，外面的热气好像全部都消散了。里面的人真多啊，仿佛就像一场聚会。有的人在看书，有的人在买书，还有的人在选书。

我和爸爸被眼前的知识的海洋吸引住了，我立刻跑去看了起来，那是一本关于植物的书，我还了其他的书。

后来我和爸爸买了很多书，还有文具、颜料、手工纸等，我们满在而归了。

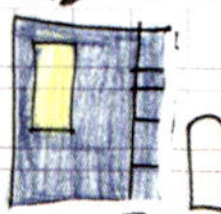

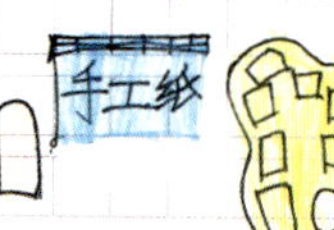

日期 2015 年 7 月 9 日　　第 1 页

登摩星岭

今天我们到了白云山的最高处——摩星岭。海拔382米，站在峰顶，不同的天气可以看到不同的景色。

我们首先到了祈愿亭，我和爸爸一起敲响了祈福钟，钟声传到很远很远。

我们又走了一段山路，突然发现路边的大树下面有三只猫在散步。那些猫一看见我，就跑过来看我，这些小猫非常可爱，我很喜欢。

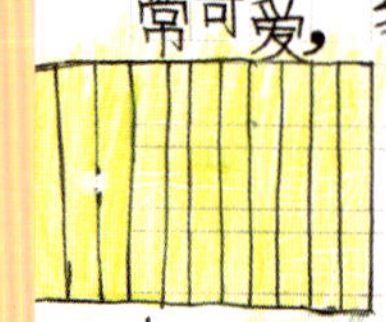

我们继续往上爬，终于爬上了摩星岭，看见整个广州市，还看见许多穿橙色衣服的人，我终于站在最高处了！

日期 2015 年 7 月 10 日　　第 2 页

抓蝴蝶

我们去了很多次白云山，看到满山飞动着美丽的蝴蝶，我非常喜欢，很想抓一只来做标本。

蝴蝶是一种灵敏的昆虫，抓它的时候，不能在前面抓，要从后面悄悄地抓才能抓的到。今天我们幸运地抓到了一只蝴蝶。

那只蝴蝶真漂亮，翅膀上的颜色有黑黄白三种颜色，以黑和黄为主色。抓到之后，我把它装在一个袋子里。

回到家后，我和爸爸把它压在书里，过几天后，就有一个新的蝴蝶标本了。

日期 2015 年 7 月 13 日　　第 3 页

寻找书中的植物

今天我们去了珠江公园玩，主要是来观察植物。

我们从南门进入公园，首先看到的是夏日紫薇，紫薇是夏天的公主。紫薇花在盛开时紫云满树，绸纱般的花瓣，一簇簇长在顶上，粉色、白色，蓝紫、翠紫，娇艳柔美的各种紫。然后我们去看了红刺露兜树，它的叶子像章鱼爪，我们找了木槿花；

山姜

露兜树

蜘蛛兰

夏日紫薇　木槿花　真假连翘

我还找到了蜘蛛兰、真假连翘、红背桂、亮叶朱蕉、长铁蕉、美人蕉、杜丽人、金山棕、杜鹃、山姜等，这些都在我的书里《早安！我的植物邻居》上面有的，今天的收获真丰富！

2015 7 14　4

带你游白云山

我是一名小导游，今天我来带你们去游览白云山。

白云山是一座名山，风景很好，有"自古羊城第一秀"的称号。它主要的景点有双溪，双溪是一个旅舍，周恩来和朱德在这里住过。麓湖公园是广州市最大的公园。鸣春谷旅游区林木葱郁，景色宜人。桃花涧是一个以观赏桃花为主的景点。《桃花源记》为构思主线的中国式山水写意园林，内设有鸿运泉、怡春亭、桃花岛、桃花源记石刻等景点。能仁寺建于清朝咸丰皇帝，建成后一度香火鼎盛，吸引了众多前来参观和朝拜的游客。摩星岭是白云山的最高峰，是个登高祈福好地方。

今天就介绍这么多了，有机会大家可以去一下白云山，亲自体验那些景色吧！

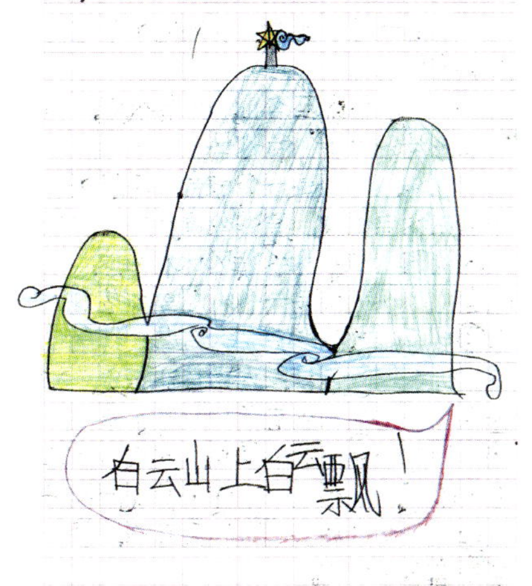

2015 7 17　5

一个开心的梦

春游了，同学们开心的叫了起来。大家都不用买面包了，因为老师这次带了锅，我们带蔬菜水果，这次大家春游的地点是火炉山。

我们先坐公交，再坐地铁，终于到火炉山。今天很凉爽，适合于郊游。

突然，一个同学说："好香的花，比玫瑰花还香！小心鼻子过敏哟，另一个同学说，这是什么植物？老师问。我说："这是珍珠野菜，又叫珍珠草，它的根可以炒来吃，它的珍珠果像珍珠一样大小，珍珠果可以用做植物油，花和叶可以用来做香水。同学赞叹道"真是一种奇特的植物！然后我们就把珍珠野菜的根炒来吃，它的根甜甜地，同学都抢着吃，吃的很开心。

啊，原来是个梦！

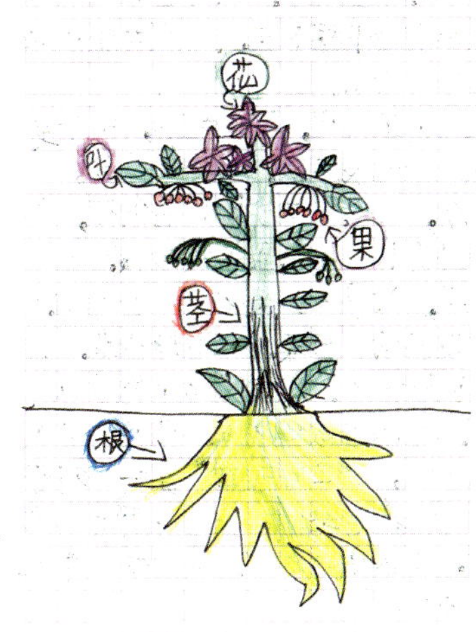

2015 7 24　6

鸣春谷中的蝴蝶和鸟

鸣春谷是白云山的一个景点，主要有科普馆、蝶舞荧飞、鸟内展览馆、我们先看了许多的蝴蝶标本，那些蝴蝶真漂亮！

我最喜欢海伦娜闪蝶，又称光明女神蝶，它是世界上最漂亮最艳丽的蝴蝶该蝶翅面底色为宝石蓝色，有强烈的金属光泽，从不同的角度看去，可以从紫蓝向天蓝、深蓝、亮蓝逐渐过渡，莫幻莫测，靓丽无比，双翅上的洁白色闪带贯穿前后翅，像镶嵌上去的珠宝。

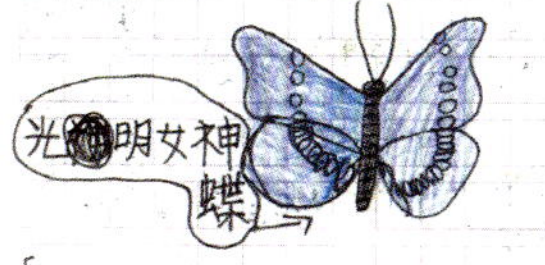

蝴蝶的生长有四个阶段，1.卵，2.幼虫，3.蛹，4.蝶。我和爸爸来到一个叫"蝶舞荧飞"的一个地方，门是用红绿、白三种颜色的铁链做地，我们进了第一个空间里，里面有花、有鱼池、有蝴蝶在飞，有蝴蝶在传粉，难怪这叫蝶舞荧飞！

离开了蝶舞荧飞这个地方，我和爸爸进了鸟内展览馆，里面的鸟有蓝孔雀、白孔雀、元宝鸡、小麻雀、蓝毛喜鹊等鸟内，我和爸爸又去了鹦鹉馆，那些鹦鹉鸟很美。然后我们又去看了小朋友抓鱼。

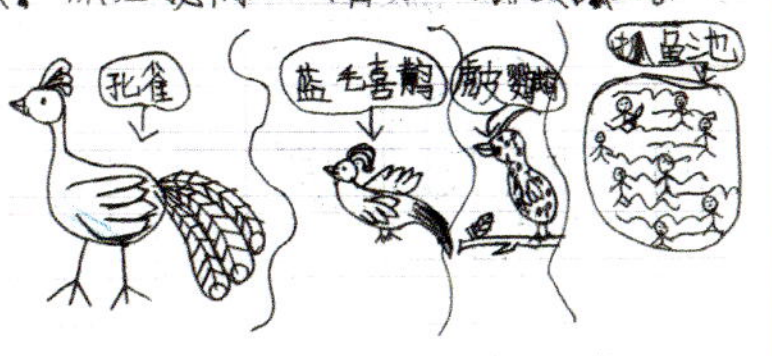

2015 8 10　7

南国书香节

南国书香节是一个很热闹的节日，许多爱阅读的人都来参加，我也在其中，因为我也爱读书，所以我就去了琶洲过"书香节"。

一开始我们下了车然后就跟着人群走，通道像蛇一样。

我们进了布房里，又是一个蛇型通道，在出口有一个领票的地方，大家领了票，就去下一个布房，布房里有一个空门，空门右边有个装包的大箱子，我们拿好自己的包，上了电梯，到了大厅，我买了三支颜色笔、三支彩色笔、一支涂改带、脑筋急转弯、野鸟观察指南、魔法森林、蝴蝶、猫咪绘，多么有意思的一天！

2015 8 18 8

小黄鱼的自诉

你好！我是一条黄色小孔雀鱼，我们出生有四阶段，1.鱼蛋，2.慢性孵化，3.完全孵化，4.出生了。

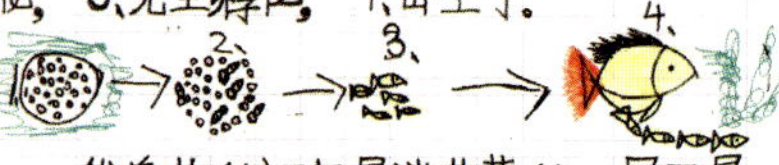

我身体的颜色是淡黄的，尾巴是淡红的。

小鱼刚出生就吃一片片的鱼饲料，因为它还小，不能吃一粒一粒的，有一天，一个人伸了一只手指，我们全都游过来吃，我的兄弟姐妹也游来吃，"怎么有那么大块肉？我怎么咬不动啊？"小鱼们问，那个人打开了认鱼图鉴，图鉴上写：这种叫小黄鱼，别名黄孔雀、五彩金、黄豆豆、麻酥金。小黄鱼想："这个人在讲什么呢？，看不懂"小黄鱼喜欢在水里玩、做游戏、追逐、游来游去、争抢食物，晚上了，太阳下山了，我睡觉！

9

火龙果

国庆见闻

周末去从化，
路上遇堵车。
堵了2小时，
肚子饿扁了。

2015年10月2日，天气：晴朗，我们一家人去了广州从化市流溪河国家森林公园去玩。去的路上遇到了大堵车，12点才到，我才发现，这是国家十大森林公园，一颗绿色明珠展现在我的眼前，那里人山人海，吃完饭后，我们坐船去了桃花岛，上岛一看，全是空空的桃树，不见有桃花。我和妈妈沿着栈道走了一圈，用了一个小时走完3公里路程，大家都夸我脚力好，我也很高兴，在回家路上，我们买了、摘了火龙果，还摘了马齿苋，我们回来了家。之后，我吃的火龙果真甜，是我亲手摘的，更甜！

内容真实有意义，将过程写出来了。我也想去流溪河公园玩！

A+
10.28

难忘的零食大会

"零食大会现在开始啦"，你想去吗？那就和我一起去教室里吧，"五年一班零食大会现在开始"主持人翟家琨说，大家欢呼起来，这一次零食大会是在我们教室下午开的，下午4:00～5:00开的。零食大会开始了，每个人都拿着自己的零食去分给别人，常元首带了各种味道的薯片，何雨甜带了小饼干和水果，而我只带了海苔还有旺仔牛奶糖，好吧。家里就只有这些食物了，我是先去刘思雨那桌分，每个人只有三片海苔两个旺仔牛奶糖。因为不多，所以我才这么想的，去完刘思雨那桌之后，就去姜正宇那桌，我给这桌的人发了零食后，想吃海苔和奶糖，就去我那桌拿来吃，这样就放心了。我也去吃东西了，肖静拿出一包烛条，男生全部都去抢。我不喜欢吃他的，所以就没去吃，翟家琨说："现在到了感恩环节，你们有什么想说的吗？

海苔

牛奶糖

薯片

葡萄干

鲜花饼

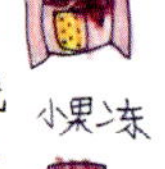

小果冻

烛条

张琪智说："有有有，我想说""那你就说吧"。"感恩的人是我的父母，因为有他（她）们，才有我这次的零食大会，后来有同学把食物丢扔到地上乱扔，这样很不好。

我的收获就是：吃要有个吃样，不然害得我们这一个学期都开不了零食大会了。

①《游悉尼和墨尔本》

"你去过澳大利亚吗？"那里的景色太美了！我们这次要去澳大利亚的两个城市，一个是悉尼，另一个是墨尔本。第一天，我去了悉尼歌剧院、圣玛丽亚大教堂、海德公园、悉尼大桥。其中，悉尼歌剧院被称为20世纪最有特色的建筑。悉尼歌剧院位于贝尼朗岬角，是丹麦建筑师约恩·乌松设计。歌剧院建成于1973年。第二天，我和妈妈一起去看房子，还去了超市里的银行。第三天，我和妈妈去了悉尼的两个大学，都是澳大利亚的八大名校。

课室里墙上挂着许多的作品，窗户上有罗马风格。校园里有：体育场、后面有游泳池，还有室内的植物园。第四天，我们去了蜡像馆和水族馆。达令港下面美丽的悉尼水族馆，馆内有来自澳洲北部大堡礁以及澳洲各个湖泊的溪流的5000多种生物。水族馆最受欢迎的是一条146米长的水底隧道，许多的鱼儿都在里面跳舞。我们离开了水底隧道，来到了大堡礁馆。

2015年2月7日 天气：晴

第五天，我们去了邦迪海滩，是澳洲最著名古老的冲浪运动中心。天气不是很好，云很多，没太阳光，人多，冲浪的人少。沙滩上有许多白色羽毛的海鸥，海鸥那么小，居然敢抢西瓜吃，还追着两个女孩抢饭盒里诱人的美食，为什么海鸥那么凶？哦！原来澳洲人很爱护动物，所以海鸥的胆子就越来越大了。

我看见沙滩上有的在冲浪，有的人在沙滩上守株待兔等太阳出来，还有人在照相，这是我们在悉尼的最后一个景点……

②完！

天气：晴 2015年2月8日

第六天，我们昨天晚上去了墨尔本，今天我们去了维多利亚艺术中心，一进门就看见了水门，好像花果山里的水帘洞，非常有趣。我们一下子去了好几个美术馆，最后我们去了现代美术馆，我还去玩了蹦蹦绳。然后我们去了袋鼠保护中心，我们先去看狸猫，我现在才发现中国的

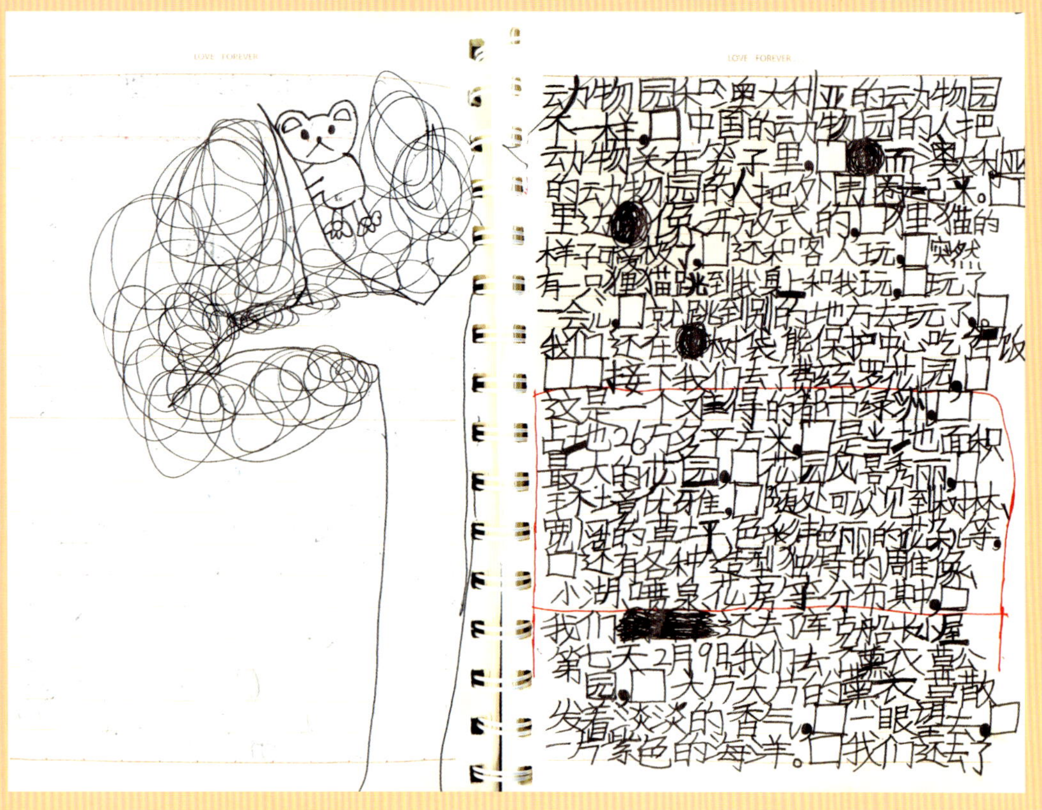

动物园和澳大利亚的动物园不一样。中国的动物园的人把动物关在笼子里。而澳大利亚的动物园的人把外围围起来。里边是开放式的。狸猫的样子可爱极了，还和客人玩。突然有一只狸猫跳到我身上和我玩。玩了一会儿，就跳到别的地方去玩了。我们还在树袋熊保护中心吃午饭。接下我们去了费兹罗花园，这是一个难得的都市绿洲，占地26万多平方米，是当地面积最大的花园。花园风景秀丽，环境优雅，随处可以见到树林、宽阔的草坪、色彩艳丽的花朵等，还有各种造型独特的雕像、小湖、喷泉、花房等分布其中。我们还去了库克船长小屋。第七天2月9日我们去了薰衣草公园。大片大片的薰衣草散发着淡淡的香气，一眼望去，一片紫色的海洋。我们还去了

葡萄庄园。那里是生产葡萄酒的地方。站在葡萄庄园还可以看到远处的大海和彩虹小屋。

③尾声

经过几天的旅程，渐渐接近尾声了。

再见，澳大利亚！

再见，墨本！

LOVE FOREVER...

文嘉年华

Kowloon Shangri-La
HONG KONG

2015年 望远镜

在香港香格里拉酒店里，我们住的是海景房，我们透过窗，看见了美丽维多利亚海港。看完之后我回到了房间。惊讶地发现房间里有一盒巧克力。一共有10个巧克力，白的3个黑的7个，3+7=10(个)！还有一个望远镜！现在是晚上，我看到了有一只金碧辉煌的灯挂在船上。望远镜可以把事物×10倍，维多利亚海港仿佛就在眼前！还有许多的灯有红、金、白、蓝、绿等颜色，灯光很像灯塔，

64 Mody Road, Kowloon, Hong Kong
Tel (852) 2721 2111 Fax (852) 2723 8686 www.shangri-la.com

LOVE FOREVER...

Kowloon Shangri-La
HONG KONG

第二天，维多利亚海港好美啊！天空灰灰的，那时候太阳还没出来，我们以为今天是阴天。于是太阳出来了！海水被照得金光闪闪！仿佛有千万亮片在水中闪着，轮船在海面上慢慢驶过。海水更蓝，太阳升得更高了！有一只轮船向岸边来了，海水把天空的颜色反射出来。天空就显得更蓝了。

望远镜，我在维多利亚海港的小伙伴！

64 Mody Road, Kowloon, Hong Kong
Tel (852) 2721 2111 Fax (852) 2723 8686 www.shangri-la.com

老师评价 Teacher's Comments

（四年级上学期）

莲子，看到这学期你的努力我真的很开心。这个学期你能主动地来问老师问题，并主动把书本交给老师批改，这是个很棒的开始。我也看出来你是一个很有创造性的孩子，你喜欢画画，每次在微信上看到你的作品都是一种享受，你很有自己的创意及想法。

——数学老师 Math

莲子，好喜欢你整齐漂亮的英文书写，还有你富有想象力的图文并茂的创意作业，课前朗读时的认真样子也特别可爱。课堂上的你稍稍显得有些安静，但有时你又会给大家带来惊喜，对于某个话题你可以大胆尝试表达自己的感受，真棒！

——英语老师 English

美术 VIP。你在绘画方面的天赋是大家所公认的，尤其是你绘画作品的构图，非常大气。画面冲击力很强，另外，你在搭配颜色方面还是一个高手，颜色不会用很多，但非常和谐、非常精准。人物头像画中的妈妈，构图大气、颜色明快；珍珠泥贴画中的向日葵，颜色虽然不多，但看起来很舒服，你真的很懂得用色，在绘画方面你绝对是个高手。

——选修课老师 Elective Course

用“静如处子动如脱兔”来形容我对莲子的印象最合适不过了。在中医推拿课上的莲子，听讲的时候是很安静的，眼睛总是跟着老师转，当我说大家自由练习的时候，莲子总会赶紧投入练习，然后迫不及待地举手问老师：“是不是这样？我这样做对吗？”得到我肯定后的莲子总会露出甜甜的笑容。课后，莲子最喜欢给我讲三国的故事，因为你，我也迷上了《三国演义》，谢谢你，博学的孩子！

——选修课老师 Elective Course

“老师，告诉你一个秘密……”

“老师，我有一个想法，就是……”

“老师，我有一个建议，你能不能……”

“老师，我有一个发现，你看……”

莲子，我的耳边经常回响起你的奇思妙想，脑海中经常浮现你纯真可爱的样子。这学期，你跟老师很亲近，时而开玩笑，时而游戏嬉闹，时而侃侃而谈。这一切让老师觉得很感动。谢谢你对我的信任与亲近。老师也悄悄跟你说一个秘密：知道我为什么这么喜欢跟你一起玩吗？因为我真的很喜欢你的真实与快乐，喜欢你的细心与上进，喜欢你的艺术气质。

莲子，我总是会很自豪地跟别人说：“莲子将来肯定是画家，我现在就想收藏她的画呢！”真的，看到你的画作后，我才感受到你的画画天赋，无论从图画的取材、构思、布局还是上色都让我赞叹不已，那种独特新颖的灵感，奔放不羁的思绪，那种淋漓尽致的画面，那种搭配完美的颜色，无不透出你的画家潜质和你画作的精彩。真的很喜欢你的画，莲子是能把画画做到极致的人，也期待你更多的作品。

——班主任老师 Master Teacher

爸爸妈妈对你说 Parent's Comment

九岁的莲子：成长为一本丰富而引人入胜的书

2014 年国庆假期，从美国回来，莲子画了一幅画《美丽花园》，写上“今天我生日！”“9 岁画”——九岁的女儿，忽然成长为一本如《美丽花园》般丰富而引人入胜的书——每天翻开，你都有新的发现，看到了意想不到的惊喜！在家里，莲子已经很熟练地分担妈妈照顾爸爸的工作，即使自己是在看书、画画，眼睛也随时留意爸爸的一举一动，并且及时提醒爸爸怎么怎么样！每当妈妈遇到难事心里着急，莲子总是想方设法开解妈妈。从美国回来，莲子笔下的图画发生了质的飞跃，对艺术的求知欲更加强烈，并且延伸到其他的学科——越来越喜欢阅读各类书籍，涉猎的范围包括古诗、国学、历史、小说、天文、地理、动植物及科幻等。

接近期末的一天，莲子回到家躲在卫生间里哭，她问妈妈：“为什么我英语考试成绩那么差呢？妈妈你给我每科都找个老师回家教我好吗？”期末，看到老师对莲子进步的鼓励和赞扬，爸爸妈妈感到无比的欣慰！寒假，莲子跟妈妈去到了澳洲，站在世界名列前茅的悉尼大学美丽的校园，莲子欢欣起舞，对妈妈说：“长大我要读悉尼大学！”宝贝，加油！只要努力，你的理想就会实现！

摘自《汇景新城实验小学学生素质发展评价表》

老师评价 Teacher's Comments

（四年级下学期）

莲子，本学期你的进步很大。刚开始时，你只是埋头做自己的事情，现在遇到困难时，会主动来找老师求助，越来越自信、大方了。找老师求助后如果答案还是错误，你也会再三尝试，从不气馁直到得到正确的答案。这就是你的成长。

——数学老师 Math

Apple, You are super polite and quiet in class and hopefully you can stay focused more often now. You are a super creative student and this creativity is what really helps you learn because you are always coming up with new things and learning in new ways. Never give up that creativity Apple, because it can take you a long way.

——英语老师 English

在科技制作中，温柔的小手拿起螺丝刀一点也不含糊，锤锤钻钻，一步一步，对于擅长画画的你，能尝试这些，真的不简单，虽然最后的作品不一定能成功，敢于尝试，并能坚持下来，这个过程让你的动手能力得到提升，你的勇气得到很多同学的认可。在实验中，你的思维灵活，常常能想到独特的办法，让大家佩服并愿意一试。

——选修课老师 Elective Course

莲子是个有很多很多精彩故事的孩子。以前总会在你的画面中欣赏到神奇的故事插图。在这学期中，英文字母设计让老师看到你故事的提升，不但画面构图新颖．还能从每一个字母中看到那么多精彩的小画面，真的很谢谢你让我又一次一饱眼福。

——选修课老师 Elective Course

亲爱的莲子：

“老师，我很喜欢莲子的！”这是同学对你的印象。

“莲子在家族很棒哟，还能照顾学妹呢！”这是史官对你的评价。

“莲子画家，画家莲子！”这是老师对你最深的感受。

四年级，我们看到了一个优秀的莲子、成长的莲子。要知道莲子是有灵性的、是能给人带来惊喜和感动的孩子。课上朗读古诗时，你字斟句酌，咬字清晰，非常有感情地读出句子，这让我们看到了你朗读的天赋。这学期看到最多的是莲子在阅读，不管是历史书，还是故事书，莲子都很喜欢，津津有味地享受其中。读书让莲子识字更多、更有想法、更有书香气质。“哇，莲子的字好漂亮啊！”每次看到你的作业老师都会赞叹不已。莲子每次写字一笔一画，认真写好，这种态度让人佩服。生活中，莲子乐于分享，每次外出都会给同学带来特产，孩子们可感激莲子了。还记得那次品尝西安美食肉夹馍，莲子觉得好吃，也帮老师拿了一块，老师很感动。

最让老师佩服的是你的绘画水平，每次看到你的作品都会情不自禁地夸赞，画得好，上色漂亮，构思新颖，布局巧妙……你美术的天赋高，老师看好你，未来的画家。老师也感谢你，因为你是我们心中的骄傲。

——班主任老师 Master Teacher

想到你，脑海里不禁浮现出你甜美的笑容。你越来越有学姐风范了，记得有一次，在用餐的你看到正准备去洗碗的学妹脸上粘了米粒，你及时地提醒她将嘴巴擦干净了再去洗碗，在你的提醒下，学妹很快就拿纸巾擦干净了嘴巴，她还走到你面前叫你看一下，你们俩相互看了看，很有默契地笑了。贴心的你，在午休起床后，当你听到老师叫学妹起床时，你就会很着急地说：“老师，让我来叫她起床吧！我有办法把她叫起来。”说完，你立刻去到学妹的床前，使出各种招数，有规规矩矩的、有小搞怪的等等，逗得其他同学都哈哈大笑。愿快乐的笑声一直陪伴在你的身边！

——生活老师 Nursing Teacher

爸爸妈妈对你说 Parent's Comment

九岁的莲子：有了自己的理想和追求

九岁的莲子，经常同妈妈讲的一句话是：“长大我要成为画家。”2015年暑假，原本计划好的意大利艺术创作之旅，却因为妈妈的原因而未能成行。虽然甚为遗憾，但莲子却能泰然处之，漫长的暑假待在家里，与鱼为伴，与花草为伴，与画为伴，与书为伴，也依然将自己的时间安排得丰富而快乐！

九岁的莲子，令父母为之惊喜的是，不仅仅艺术创作更加丰富、有了质的飞跃，而且对中国历史以及《三国演义》的人物及故事更是滚瓜烂熟，对大自然的热爱也令她成了植物“百科全书”。但妈妈也想告诉莲子的一句话是：如果女儿长大想读悉尼大学，那就必须成长为全面发展的孩子哦！宝贝，为了实现自己的理想，加油！

摘自《汇景新城实验小学学生素质发展评价表》

奖状

程莲子

在2014-2015学年第一学期中，表现突出，成绩优秀，荣获快乐分享天使奖。

特发此状，以资鼓励！

慎思·笃学　厚德·博雅

匯景新城實驗小學
Favorview Palace Primary School
2015年1月20日

奖状

程莲子

在2014-2015学年第一学期中，表现突出，成绩优秀，荣获绘画构图色彩大师奖。

特发此状，以资鼓励！

慎思·笃学　厚德·博雅

匯景新城實驗小學
Favorview Palace Primary School
2015年1月20日

奖状

程莲子

在2014-2015学年第一学期中，表现突出，成绩优秀，荣获硬笔书法家奖。

特发此状，以资鼓励！

慎思·笃学　厚德·博雅

匯景新城實驗小學
Favorview Palace Primary School
2015年1月20日

奖状

程莲子

在2014-2015学年第一学期中，表现突出，成绩优秀，荣获好学上进奖。

特发此状，以资鼓励！

慎思·笃学　厚德·博雅

匯景新城實驗小學
Favorview Palace Primary School
2015年1月20日

奖状

程莲子

在2014-2015学年第二学期中，表现突出，成绩优秀，荣获书香才女奖。

特发此状，以资鼓励！

慎思·笃学　厚德·博雅

匯景新城實驗小學
Favorview Palace Primary School
2015年7月6日

奖状

程莲子

在2014-2015学年第二学期中，表现突出，成绩优秀，荣获硬笔书法家奖。

特发此状，以资鼓励！

慎思·笃学　厚德·博雅

匯景新城實驗小學
Favorview Palace Primary School
2015年7月6日

奖状

程莲子

在2014-2015学年第二学期中，表现突出，成绩优秀，荣获绘画高手奖。

特发此状，以资鼓励！

慎思·笃学　厚德·博雅

匯景新城實驗小學
Favorview Palace Primary School
2015年7月6日

编后记

十岁女孩的世界

十岁女孩的世界有多大？看看这本《童心无限》便可知晓。

程莲子是一个十岁女孩，这本画册收集了她十年来大量的绘画作品、摄影作品、生活照片和各阶段老师的评语、父母的寄语等资料，形象而艺术地展现了一个十岁女孩的成长足迹和艺术学习的历程，将她十年间各阶段的心灵世界和艺术感觉展现得完整而生动，其洋溢的天真和童趣让人忍俊不禁，同时又不得不令人由衷生发出“童心无限”的感叹！

童心之无限，仅从绘画作品就可以看得出来。程莲子从两岁开始涂鸦作画，九年来可谓笔耕不辍，用她无师自通的色彩和线条，涂抹和描画了2000多张画图，这本画册仅选出来的一部份，便将一个小姑娘可以观察和想象的世界展现得千奇百怪、多彩缤纷，有些表现方法和主题甚至是我们这些成年人所匪夷所思、不得其解的。一些色彩各异的乱笔涂抹，她说是“海底动物”；两个怪模怪样的人形，她说是“妈妈和宝宝”；她还会用三十多个画面将在美国旅游的全过程做成“连环画”；她在那个年龄段读过的童话故事和所看过的动画片几乎都可以在她的画中找到其中的人物、角色……

这些作品，如果用现成的艺术标准来评价其技法，是没有意义的，因为她还没有受过完整的专业训练，还不可能套入那些公式化的技法标准中，但这并不影响她在作品中所展现的无限的艺术想象力，由于这些想象力没有任何约定俗成的观念禁锢，没有任何公式化的技法束缚，因而显得那样恣肆无忌，无边无垠，犹如天马行空，自由洒脱，而这往往是成年人所缺少并求之不得的。成年人通常看重技法，但需知任何一种技法在带来精确和娴熟的同时，也都意味着规矩和束缚，而任何规矩和束缚对艺术的创新性和个性来说，都是抑多于扬、弊多于利的。

而小孩子却不一样，他们可能没有掌握技巧，但在他们的眼中，世界是五颜六色的，生活是多姿多彩的，他们通过尚未沾染人情世故的清澈双眸去观察和理解，通过无比旺盛的激情去发现和体验，通过没有任何拘束的方式去描画和表现，这些，正是艺术创作不竭的源泉，是创新性和个性化作品得以产生的最重要的基础。

“为了像一个6岁的小孩子那样作画，我学了整整一辈子。”世界艺术大师毕加索作画一生，到老年时悟出了这样一个画理，启人深思。它告诉我们：就艺术本初的意义来讲，每一个孩子都可以是艺术大师，因为艺术最需要的是无拘无束的想象力和可供挥洒的自由空间，而小孩子往往不缺这个。程莲子的画作，真实而形象地印证了这个道理。

说到程莲子的成长，不得不提到她的家庭。她的父亲本身就是一个画家，以画荷花而闻名，莲子有样学样，才一岁多就会爬上父亲的画台在宣纸上抓笔涂抹，长期的耳濡目染培养了她画画的兴趣。莲子的母亲爱好艺术和收藏，尤为重视培养她的艺术感受力和想象力，经常带她去国内外著名的艺术区和画展现场游览参观，北京、香港、新加坡、澳洲、美国等地的著名博物馆、美术馆、艺术区以及各种国际性艺术大展，都留下了她童年的足迹和好奇的目光。正是在这样的家庭氛围中，莲子像一株艺术小苗，接受艺术的阳光雨露滋养，伸枝长叶，茁壮成长。在《童心无限》中，这种饱含艺术色彩的亲情照片在各个年龄段均可看到，从中不难领会父母对莲子的艺术期盼和拳拳爱心。

在编辑《童心无限》这本画册时，程莲子小朋友参与了全部作品及照片的筛选以及拟名等工作，并且由她本人最后定稿，当我们与小画家的意见有不同时，我们充分尊重她本人的意见，旨在编辑的这本画册是能够还原其难能可贵的童真、童趣。画册的出版，得到了著名美术评论家、中国国家博物馆研究馆员朱万章博士的热心支持，为本画册写下了爱心洋溢的序言，在此表示衷心的感谢！并且，感谢汇景新城国际幼儿园杨渊园长和汇景新城实验小学程莲子的班主任刘丽君老师、广东美术馆培训中心黄子君老师、左清老师等人，对画册的资料收集提供了大力的支持。同时，非常感谢黄子君老师和香港联合出版集团符俊杰先生对画册的设计提供了许多指导性建议，以及符俊杰先生、香港理工大学英语系李蓝副教授对全书的英文翻译给予了宝贵的意见。还有，广东明星国际文化传播公司的陈怡菲、黄志威、甄文彪等人参加了全书的资料整理、英文翻译、图片编辑等工作，对他们的辛勤劳动在此一併表示谢意！

最后，还特别代程莲子的父母向汇景新城国际幼儿园莲子的老师和杨渊园长、汇景新城实验小学莲子的班主任刘丽君老师、刘晓秋老师和詹文龄校长、刘晓春校长、梁彩宁校长以及广东美术馆培训中心黄子君老师、史方方校长等众多的老师们致谢，衷心感谢你们在程莲子成长的路上所给予的辛勤付出和温暖的爱，让莲子能够在充满阳光的日子里茁壮成长！

十岁女孩的世界有多大？这本《童心无限》告诉你：想象力有多大，世界就有多大！我们也相信，程莲子通过她丰富的艺术想象力和持续努力，必将走向更为广阔的艺术世界。

张建平

2015 年 12 月

《童心无限》编辑讨论会

Afterword

The World of a Ten-Year-Old Girl

How big is the world of a ten-year-old girl? You will know after reading the book, *Boundless Imagination of a Child*.

Cheng Lianzi is a ten-year-old girl. This picture album contains a large number of her paintings, photography works, photos of daily life and comments from her teachers of various stages and a letter from her parents, etc. This book records the traces of the ten-year-old girl's growth and painting study in a vivid and artistic manner. In this album, we can see a complete and dynamic description of her inner world and art talent of different stages over the past decade. The innocence and child interest might make you laugh while feeling that the child's imagination is so limitless.

The paintings will tell you how boundless a child's imagination can be. Cheng Lianzi has been drawing pictures since she was two years old. And she has been keeping this interest for the following nine years without interruption. With her self-developed style of line and color usage, Lianzi created more than 2000 pieces of graffiti and paintings, part of which are collected in this album. The selected pictures are enough to present a curious and colorful world perceived or imagined by a little girl. Some ways and topics of her expression are so inconceivable that even adults like us are not able to interpret. For example, some colorful graffiti are claimed to be "Undersea Animals" ; two curiously shaped figures are named "Mom and Baby". She even tried to create a picture-story book with about thirty pictures about her tour in the U.S. Almost all figures/roles of fairy tales and animated films for her age to read can be found in her paintings.

The painting skills, however, should not be estimated by the existing artistic standards. There is no point in doing so because she has not yet received sophisticated professional training. So her works would not be in accordance with those standardized drawing techniques. Her free expression of imagination about art has never been hindered. Without conventional constraints and formulated drawing skills, her imagination appeared so free and boundless, just like a horse galloping in the sky. Imagination is what adult artists need but lack, for they generally emphasize skills. Needless to say, techniques incur rules and restraints but boost accuracy and proficiency. Any form of rules and restraints are believed to do more harm than good to novel and individual artistic creations.

Children are different. They might not be equipped with skills, but they see a colorful world and life through their unstained eyes. They discover and experience the world with full passion. They draw and present without any limitation. All these are inexhaustible sources of artistic creations and the most important foundations for novelty and individuality.

"To paint like a six-year-old kid, I used my whole lifetime." said the world-renowned artist Picasso. This though-provoking enlightenment was what he concluded about painting at an old age. He taught us a good moral: In a primary sense, every child is a great artist because he has boundless imagination and more freedom of expressions, both of which are required of real art. The paintings of Cheng Lianzi are the exact reflection of such notion.

The growth of Cheng Lianzi cannot be separated from her family. Her father is a professional painter famous for drawing lotus. Lianzi followed her father's step on the path. When she was only one year old, she used to climb onto her father's desk, grasp a paintbrush and began to draw as she liked. Her interest in drawing was developed under such direct influence of her father over a long time. Lianzi's mother, who is a lover of art and collection, attaches great importance to cultivating her daughter's sense of art and imagination. Therefore, she took Lianzi to famous art zones and exhibitions both home and abroad frequently. Thus, Lianzi left her footprints and curious eyesight in many museums, galleries, art zones and all kinds of artist exhibitions in places like Beijing, Hongkong, Singapore, Australia, the United States, etc. It is such a favorable family environment that has enabled Lianzi to grow like a small tree, with the sunshine and rainfall of art. The tree is stretching out branches and growing vigorously now. Photos of different times of the family can be seen in the book *Boundless Imagination of a Child*. From the book you may know her parents' high expectations and deep love for her.

During the process of editing the picture album, Cheng Lianzi, our little heroine, has taken part in selecting, finalizing and naming all the pictures and photos included in this album. When different opinions occur between the little painter and the editing staff, Lianzi's ideas were fully respected, so that the picture album preserves the innocence and interest of a child. The publishing of this album has been kindly assisted by Dr. Zhu Wanzhang, famous art critic and Researcher of the National Museum. Thanks shall be extended to Dr.Zhu for writing the preface for the book with great sincerity. Yang Yuan (Principal of Huijing New Town International Kindergarten), Liu Lijun (Class Teacher of Lianzi in Huijing New Town Experimental Primary school), Huang Zijun and Zuo Qing (teachers from Training Center of Guangdong Museum of Art) shall also be thanked for their great support in collecting materials for this picture album. Meanwhile, the instructive suggestions from teacher Huang Zijun and Mr. Fu Junjie (of Sino United Publishing (Holdings) Limited) are highly appreciated. Also, Mr. Fu Junjie and Li Lan (Associate Professor of English Department of Hong Kong Polytechnic University) has provided valuable advices to the translation of this book. Staff of Guangdong Star International Culture Media—Chen Yifei, Huang Zhiwei, Zhen Wenbiao—have been involved in the processing of materials, translation and photo editing with tremendous efforts, are also highly appreciated.

Finally, on behalf of the parents of Cheng Lianzi, I would like to thank all the teachers and Headmaster (Yang Yuan) of Huijing New Town Kindergarten, the class teachers (Liu Lijun, Liu Xiaoqiu) and Headmasters (Zhan Wenling, Liu Xiaochun, Liang Caining) in Huijing New Town Experimental Primary School, the teacher (Huang Zijun) and Headmaster (Shi Fangfang) in the training center of Guangdong Art Museum. Thank you for your sincere love and care for Lianzi to make her life full of sunshine on her way of growing up.

How large is the world of a ten-year-old girl? The picture album will tell you: The world can be as big as you can imagine. We also believe that Cheng Lianzi will have a larger world of art with her rich imagination and perseverance.

Zhang Jianping
December, 2015